Jacquard square woven in a Macclesfield garret

Eileen M Hedley
with love from
Louanne

Eileen T Hedley
love
Moira

Silk

SARSENETS, SATINS, STEELS & STRIPES

150 YEARS OF MACCLESFIELD TEXTILE DESIGNS

BY

LOUANNE COLLINS AND MOIRA STEVENSON

WITH AN INTRODUCTION BY

MARY SCHOESER

PUBLISHED BY MACCLESFIELD MUSEUMS TRUST REGISTERED CHARITY NO.519521

ISBN No: 1 870926 04 8

Preface

This publication is not intended to be an exhaustive and comprehensive account of the Macclesfield textile production. A great deal more research is necessary before this could be possible. The aim of this work is to bring the attention of historians, students and the wider public to the existence of the material in public and private collections which provides the evidence of the great variety and quality of production achieved by the Macclesfield manufacturers.

Macclesfield's connections with silk go back to the 16th century and there are documentary sources which claim that broad silk weaving was established in the town as early as the 1750s. However, this publication has concentrated on the last 150 years, 1840 - 1990, as this is the period represented in the collections of pattern books.

During the establishment of the two Silk Museums in Macclesfield, which took place between 1982 and 1987, much work was done on the organisational, social, economic and technological aspects of the silk industry in Macclesfield. Surveys of the textile mills, dyehouses and weavers' garrets were undertaken One of the areas which the Macclesfield Museum Trust felt merited further attention in 1992 was that of textile design. The opportunity to undertake a survey of the Macclesfield textile designs which have survived in public and private collections arose when the Pilgrim Trust offered grants via the Museum and Galleries Commission. The Museum made a successful grant application and Mary Schoeser was appointed to undertake the survey; Sue Guy acted as research assistant, and the Museum Curator, Louanne Collins, provided guidance and direction.

The survey aimed to cover pattern books in public and private collections. The two main public collections are housed at Macclesfield Museums and Cheshire County Record Office but miscellaneous books at the Victoria and Albert Museum and the Whitworth Art Gallery were also viewed.

The private collections were essentially those of three major firms who had retained their own collections: Adamley Textiles, James Arnold and Company and Barracks Fabrics. In total these collections comprised 750 books representing the designs of 14 manufacturers. In addition there were many thousands of samples and designs in the Silk Museum collections which have been established since 1982. These individual samples did not form part of the survey but a selection of them feature in this publication which aims to combine the knowledge of Macclesfield textile designs with other documentary evidence which has been derived from the Museum archives and previous research. It is hoped that the publication will serve to stimulate interest in the textiles from Macclesfield and encourage further research.

Acknowledgements

The Trustees of Macclesfield Museum Trust wish to thank the Pilgrim Trust and Museums and Galleries Commission who funded the initial survey by Mary Schoeser and Sue Guy. They also convey their grateful appreciation to the following bodies who have funded the printing of this publication: The North West Museums Service, Cheshire County Council, Macclesfield Borough Council, The Friends of Macclesfield Silk Heritage and The Worshipful Company of Weavers.

The Trustees acknowledge the support of the public and private institutions who allowed access to their collections and the individuals whose co-operation greatly assisted the smooth running of the project –

Adamley Textiles : Marian and Alex Adamski,

Eric Hockenhull and Michael Bateson,

Barracks Fabrics : Michael Holmes, Sue Magee, Malcolm Sherratt

James Arnold & Co. : John Arnold and Caleb Newington

Cheshire County Record Office: Jonathan Peplar and staff

The Trustees also express their appreciation to the authors.

The authors thank Barbara Arthur for her hard work and patience in typing the manuscript. Thanks and appreciation are also due to the photographer Christopher Johnson for working in difficult conditions to achieve excellent results.

Front Cover: Macclesfield Stripe handkerchiefs 1930s
End Papers: Jacquard woven 'steel' John Barlow c1902

Contents

TITLE PAGE   3

PREFACE   4

ACKNOWLEDGEMENTS   5

INTRODUCTION   8

THE DEVELOPMENT OF THE INDUSTRY   12

DESIGN AND DESIGNERS   20

FIBRES AND FABRICS   32

DYEING AND PRINTING   37

CUSTOMERS   40

MENSWEAR   48

WOMENSWEAR   56

SILK PICTURES AND EPHEMERA   64

NON FASHION USES   66

KNITTING   68

TRIMMINGS   72

COLLECTIONS   74

DIRECTORY OF FIRMS   75

GLOSSARY   82

FURTHER READING   83

Cravat sample woven using a swivel shuttle J & T Brocklehurst c1850

Introduction

Today associated with 'boiling silks' and 'small neats', the Macclesfield silk industry was and is much more diverse, encompassing the gamut of design styles - from elegant to whimsical - and a broad range of production techniques. In part this may be because from the outset Macclesfield's trading contacts were equally wide. The modest beginning some 400 years ago as a centre for thread-covered button making encouraged trading links with London that were strengthened by the introduction of narrow ribbons, braids and tapes in the mid 1600s. From beyond Britain came the raw silk itself, as well as French and Flemish weavers in the 1600s, and water-powered silk throwing from Italy in the 1740s. An international outlook was therefore well-established by the mid-1700s, when dyeing (both plain and patterned) and silk broad-cloth weaving (including ginghams and damasks) were recorded in the region. This outlook was strengthened throughout the 1800s as Macclesfield began to export finished cloths and rose to prominence as a centre for the throwing, weaving and printing of silk.

The rise of Macclesfield was tied in several ways to the rise and fall of the East London weavers, whose sumptuous hand-woven products of the 1700s made their borough, Spitalfields, synonymous with fine fashion silks. Initially Macclesfield throwsters prospered by making silk yarns for Spitalfields' weavers, but with the growing preference in the 1770s and 1780s for simpler styles (and so simpler cloths), Spitalfields' weavers lost their pre-eminence. Much depleted in number by wage disputes and the fluctuations of trade (the latter a factor to affect all silk centres), Spitalfields' weavers carried on in gradually declining conditions throughout the 1800s and early 1900s, during which time many weavers left the area. Because broad cloth weaving was established in Macclesfield just as Spitalfields entered a decline, it was well placed to satisfy the demand for relatively plain lustrous silks - a fashion that prevailed into the mid 1800s. During this period Macclesfield became known for its silk handkerchief and scarf production, while at the same time consolidating its importance as the chief centre of production for silk weaving yarns. Sir Frank Warner in "The Silk Industry" noted that in each week of 1834-35 Manchester looms alone absorbed about 8000 lbs of Macclesfield thrown silk.

The diversity of Macclesfield 's production by the mid 1800s is also noted in Warner's account, which cites a local directory listing not only 540 garret weavers, 86 manufacturers (that is, with weavers gathered into mills), 18 trimming, gimp and fringe firms and 56 throwsters, but also silk brokers, merchants, waste dealers, dyers and printers. Such diversity - all based mainly on silk - set Macclesfield apart from other centres such as Coventry, where, by

Spitalfields

Paradise Street, Macclesfield

the 1860s, the weaving of silk ribbons was already being replaced as a major employment by the weaving of elastic webbing, wool and cotton and the manufacture of sewing machines. The other major silk area in North Essex/South East Suffolk (centred on Braintree) prospered through the years between 1860 and 1920 by specialising in fine furnishing fabrics (Daniel Walters & Sons and Warner & Sons) and crepe (Courtaulds).

The presence of all stages of manufacture in Macclesfield provided a buffer against the vagaries of trade and allowed both old and new technologies to survive. Looking at the 1890s as an example, one could find hand and power looms, Jacquard, swivel and dobby looms, knitting machines, and a range of printing and dyeing methods - from flat copperplate printing and tie-dye to direct and resist hand block printing, the latter supported by the largest collection of blocks in the country. Printing not only used silks made in the town, but created another avenue for innovation, such as the invention in about 1901 of mitred blocks for scarf printing, the use of a German method of batik techniques during the 1920s, or the introduction of hand screen printing in the late 1920s (the latter spawning a screen-making business). And, although known as a silk town, from the early button-making - when worsted was incorporated with silk - Macclesfield manufacturers to the present day have dealt with other fibres. Records from the early 1800s indicate that cotton was being processed in the town, and in about 1900 man-made fibres were introduced with the aid of Comte Hilaire de Chardonnet, who launched the first successful nitro-cellulose rayon at the Paris Exhibition of 1889. Later, synthetic fibres were to play an important part in the growth and sustenance of the local textile industry.

The breadth of skills honed in Macclesfield had wide-ranging implications. The American silk industry developed in the 1860s and 1870s largely as a result of Macclesfield emigrants; during the same decades James Ford ran the Macclesfield School of Art, emigrating in 1881 for an equivalent position in Cape Town, South Africa. Sir Thomas Wardle of Leek, who introduced William Morris to indigo dyeing and the use of Indian wild, or Tussah, silk in England, had part of his technical training in Macclesfield and designers trained locally also became an important commodity, particularly once they were examined in the 1870s-1890s by the most prominent designers of the day: Owen Jones, William Morris, Walter Crane and Lewis F Day. Aside from serving as in-house designers, creating styles for markets as diverse as Rangoon, Paris and New York , Macclesfield freelance design firms served the industry at large. Others left to make substantial contributions elsewhere: Bertrand

Handloom weaving Cartwright & Sheldon 1933

Powerloom weaving

Ladies Jacquard woven neck handkerchief from the Nicholson designs

Whittaker and Herbert Woodman both left Macclesfield (in 1908 and 1920 respectively) for 40 year long careers as designers for Warners. Throughout this century British firms have benefited from Macclesfield skills, whether studio block printers such as Joyce Clissold, who prized Macclesfield plain silks as a surface to work on, or design-led companies such as Cresta, Ascher, Berne Silks or the more contemporary English Eccentrics, Collier Campbell, Liberty and Timney Fowler, all of whom had designs produced in the town.

Today but a fraction of its former size, Macclesfield silk manufacturing still retains the ingredients that have made it unique, diverse and flexible. Yarn processing, plain and Jacquard weaving, hand and machine printing, and teams of designers continue to serve an international market, while hand weaving survives under the umbrella of the Macclesfield Museums Trust. Also surviving are representative records of the industry over the past 150 years, unique not only by virtue of the range of techniques they document, but also because the great majority remain within the County to be consulted in tandem with the excellent social history and architectural surveys conducted in recent years by the Museum. The pattern books document the wide range of designs produced in the district both for home and overseas markets and so provide a guide to the changing international tastes in fashion fabrics and accessories. They also prove that 'boiling silks' and 'small neats' (both developments of the 1920s and 1930s) are just a minute part of Macclesfield's history.

Detail from a Timney Fowler shawl 1988

'Neat' tie design 1934–35 shows different colourways

The Development of the Industry

Macclesfield, on the banks of the River Bollin, is situated where the Pennine Hills meet the Cheshire Plain. It developed and thrived as a market town on the north-south route allowing easy access to the Midlands and London, whilst the east-west route provided links with Derbyshire and Chester. In the Middle Ages it was the administrative centre of Macclesfield Forest, a royal hunting ground, and of the Manor of Macclesfield and the Macclesfield Hundred. In 1261 King Edward I granted a Charter to the town.

In the 16th century considerable numbers of sheep grazed the extensive forest lands to the east of Macclesfield but a true woollen industry never prospered.

Button making developed as a cottage industry to augment the livelihood of the predominantly subsistence farmers. Early buttons were fairly coarse and consisted of wooden moulds covered either with hair from horses and oxen or with linen thread. Holly wood, mentioned in inventories of the 16th century, is likely to have been the preferred material for the moulds especially as it is known that holly trees grew in abundance in the area, for example in that district of Macclesfield known as 'The Hollins'. In 1574 a debt was entered in the town accounts for "Buttonz and for making buttonz of ye value of 15s". In the same year the Mayor and Burgesses passed an order regulating the button trade, by which no strangers were allowed to infringe on the tradesmen's monopoly of button making.

Silk had been worked in England on a small scale since the Middle Ages and ecclesiastical work known as 'Opus Angelicanum' was of a high quality. The industry was greatly stimulated by the influx of Huguenot and Flemish refugees escaping religious persecution.

The earliest known reference to silk in Macclesfield is recorded in the inventory of silk button man, Stephen Rowe, drawn up in 1617. He operated his business on the 'putting out' system. His will lists quantities of raw materials including silk and moulds and reveals significant links with London. He also had agricultural interests.

During the 17th century the Macclesfield button making industry increased in importance. In 1698 the Corporation directed that "poor children or other poor should be instructed in the making of buttons or other matters relating to the trade".

Diversification into yarn preparation began in the middle of the 17th century with the invention of machines for winding silk and for making silk twist. The silk waste from the twisting process, unsuitable for broad silk manufacture, was woven into narrow fabrics or smallwares. The introduction into the town in

1737 of the Dutch Engine Loom firmly established narrow fabric weaving, producing galloons, doubles and ferrets.

The majority of the buttons and smallwares were carried out of the immediate area by mounted chapmen often as far as London, thus the Macclesfield silk industry forged early links with the capital. Despite competition from areas which produced buttons or other materials more cheaply, the silk and mohair buttons from Macclesfield survived into the 19th century.

The first textile factory in Britain was built in Derby by John and Thomas Lombe in 1718. It was a silk throwing mill, based on Italian technology. When the patent expired in 1732 other mills quickly followed and in 1744 Charles Roe established a water powered throwing mill in Macclesfield. Within a short time another 12 mills had been built in the town. Raw silk was sent from London for throwing and the yarn was returned to Spitalfields.

According to John Prout, a Macclesfield weaver, who published "A Practical View of the Silk Trade" in 1829, broad loom weaving commenced in 1756 with the manufacture of calgees and black fringes. The manufacture made little progress until 1780 when Mr C Beswick "advanced a step in it" and calgees, now woven with a soft, rather than a hard warp and shute, were known as bandannas. However, John Corry writing in 1817 credits the first manufacture to Leigh & Voce, weaving in Back Street from 1790. From this date until the end of the Napoleonic Wars the Macclesfield industry flourished.

In the late 1700s the silk trade was a handwork industry carried out in the workers' cottages. The houses, known as garrets, comprised 3 storeys, with the workshop on the top floor. Most loom shops above the living quarters were approached by ladder through a trapdoor and had to have a large ceiling height to accommodate the looms. Over 600 garret houses have been identified in Macclesfield (although not all of them were used for weaving).

The master weaver or undertaker who rented or owned the house might have weavers and apprentices working there for him, together with all the members of the family.

There were 2 systems of apprenticeship in Macclesfield: 'Domestic Apprentices' received bed and board whilst 'Half Pay' apprentices lived at home and were paid a weekly wage of half what their labour earned.

Between 1800 and 1831 the population of Macclesfield expanded from 8743 to 23129. This period saw a massive increase in the building of mills and workers' housing. In 1814 there were 30 mills; 10 years later there were 70.

Certificate awarded on completion of 7 year weaving apprenticeship 1819

SILK FERRET, GALLOON, TWIST & HAT-BAND MANFRS.
Barber Timothy, Bank top
Brooke James, Beach lane
Brunt Joseph, George & William, Sunderland street [Stanley st
Moss George, Abraham and Isaac,
Mottershead Cath. Parsonage st

Pigot's Directory 1850

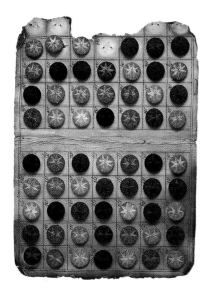

Macclesfield silk and mohair buttons manufactured by
J & T Brocklehurst

18th century button maker *from Diderot*

The outworkers began to lose their status with the advent of the factory
system. The manufacturers felt that standards in the mill were higher and the
weavers were easier to regulate. Strict timekeeping was adhered to and even if
a minute or two late a worker was liable to be locked out. The 'knocker up'
was a familiar sight round town tapping on the bedroom windows.

The Jacquard mechanism invented in about 1800 was introduced to
Macclesfield in the 1820s, having been brought to the North West by a
Frenchman, Devoge, who had probably worked with Jacquard. Powerlooms
were also used in the mills in the 1820s. At first they were unsuitable for silk
and progress was slow, but by the middle of the century powerloom weaving
was gradually taking over from weaving on handlooms.

Wages in the Macclesfield silk industry were generally low. In 1793 the
average wage in a good spell was 15s 1d (£0.75) per week for men and in
1825, 19s 7d (£0.97) In 1912 men could earn up to 30 shillings (£1.50) and
women up to 20 shillings (£1.00).

The majority of silk workers were women and Macclesfield was always
known as a 'women's town'. However, all the supervisory and skilled jobs were
reserved for men, who were usually paid more. The only skilled positions

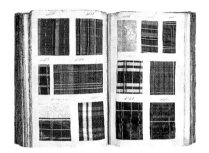

Tartans woven by J & T Brocklehurst

18th century handloom weaving *from Diderot*

available to women were warping and later powerloom weaving. Soldiers returning after the Napoleonic Wars created a glut in labour. At the same time Britain lost its American and European markets to France and Italy who could produce high quality goods at a cheaper price. The Silk Masters proposed a 25% reduction in wages and that the weavers should be paid for producing bandannas by weight rather than quantity, resulting in a further reduction in wages. The weavers went on strike but eventually had to accept the new terms, which included doing away with fixed prices. Despite the depression in trade after the Napoleonic Wars the industry continued to prosper. In 1825 the Macclesfield Courier and Herald wrote "So flourishing is this most important manufacture that it is impossible to keep pace with the demand for goods".

By the end of 1825 another depression was being keenly felt in Macclesfield. The Government had decided to adopt a policy of Free Trade in order to "extend the foreign trade of the country". The trade depression worsened and in 1832 a Committee of Enquiry was set up to investigate the problems facing the silk trade. Macclesfield was represented by manufacturers, weavers and throwsters, all of whom testified to the hardships endured by the industry.

Richard Cobden

John Prout, a weaver, wrote in 1832 "I have seen my children surrounding the table, and heard their cries for food, embittered with the reflection that I had none to give them".

Children were employed in the mills as a source of cheap labour, first in the throwing processes and then in weaving. Advertisements in the Macclesfield Courier in the early 1820s show that demand for child labour was high. The Poor Law Authorities were encouraged to send workhouse children to the mills.

In the early 19th century there were few regulations about the age at which children could start work and the number of hours to be worked. Even when the Factory Act of 1833 improved conditions of employment, the silk industry was treated differently and children under 13 worked a 10 hour day and a 60 hour week and an education could only be obtained by attending Sunday School.

The 1851 census for Macclesfield showed that 86.7% of girls under 15 were employed in the textile industry (mainly silk). In 1875 the Factory Act made 10 years the minimum age for half time employment on the production of an exemption certificate stating that certain education standards had been met, and full time employment could begin at 13. In 1873, 6380 young people under 16 worked in the Macclesfield silk industry. In 1918 half-timers earned 2s 6d (12¹/₂p) per week. After 1918 it was compulsory to attend full time education between 5 and 14.

The Cheshire silk industry employed over 22000 people in 1851, mainly concentrated in and around the towns of Macclesfield and Congleton. However, the industry which had suffered so severely in the depressions of

Throwing by hand 18th century

1826 and 1832 was still very vulnerable to outside influences. The Silk Weavers Committee report in the Macclesfield Courier for January 1858 stated that the Committee had relieved 19000 cases by the issue of rations in either soup, bread, rice or tea. On 6 February the Committee reported that although there was more employment the pressure on the unemployed was still very severe. Another 60 tons of coal and £10 worth of clogs was voted as "they are much sought after". The Cobden Treaty with France in 1860 finally removed trade barriers, thus allowing the import of cheaper, but high quality goods, which proved disastrous to the British silk industry.

In order to relieve the unemployment situation emigration was encouraged to Australia, New Zealand and particularly Patterson, New Jersey (the home of the American Silk Industry founded by John Ryle, a Macclesfield man).

Firms that had survived the booms and slumps of the first half of the 19th century improved their technology and diversified their products. Whilst the majority of work was now carried on in the mills, some outwork continued, particularly for short runs and specialist work. The garrets associated with James Arnold & Co continued until the 1940s. Handloom weaving continued in a limited way until the last handloom weaver retired when the firm of Cartwright and Sheldon closed in 1981.

The silk industry briefly recovered at the beginning of the 20th century as firms adapted their machinery to weave artificial silk. In the 1920s the introduction of a washing silk for everyday wear known as 'Macclesfield Stripe' brought renewed business for the Macclesfield silk industry.

As with many others, the industry had fixed holidays, with Barnaby in June and Wakes in October. Recreation included the carnival with the crowning of

18th century water powered throwing machinery *from Diderot*

Macclesfield c1820

the Silk Queen as the high spot, and most firms had their own jazz bands. These traditions were curtailed by the 1939-1945 War.

During the Second World War Macclesfield became the centre for the supply of silk and all available silk was requisitioned for the war effort. Some firms were fully employed weaving parachutes in silk. After the war the industry steadily contracted with the remaining firms mostly weaving artificial silk; with only a small portion of production using natural fibres. Macclesfield firms were always in the forefront in the development of new products, for example working with ICI on the early production of nylon. The club tie industry became the staple product and Macclesfield today continues to be a centre for tie manufacture with some weaving and printing on silk.

Macclesfield from The Hollins c1850

Design Education

The first evidence of art or design training in the town dates from 1833 when the evening classes organised in upper rooms in Puddingbag Street (now Lower Exchange Street) by the manager of the Macclesfield Sunday School featured drawing among the subjects offered. These classes were then continued by the Useful Knowledge Society which was established in 1835 with the support and encouragement of Mr John Brocklehurst MP, a member of the silk manufacturing family. John Brocklehurst had spoken at the first public meeting held in the Town Hall on the 8th May 1835 to discuss "the expediency of forming a society for the Diffusion of Useful Knowledge amongst the operatives connected with the town and trade of Macclesfield". A month later, on 12th June, a further meeting was held that John Brocklehurst was not able to attend having been detained in London. However, he sent a letter to be read out at the meeting in which he states "I attended a deputation of the gentlemen connected with the silk trade of Coventry yesterday at the Board of Trade; and amongst other topics under discussion was the grant of a sum of money to enable them to establish a school of design whereby to improve their taste in the manufacture of ribbons."

It is clear from this that Macclesfield was aware of the discussions which were going on nationally with regard to the establishment of schools of design and the Committee of Arts and Manufactures which was set up in 1835 "to enquire into the best means of extending a knowledge of the Arts and principles of design among the people (especially the manufacturing population) of the Country". This concern was inspired by a general consensus amongst intellectuals, industrialists and working men that British design compared badly with that of European competitors. This was particularly felt in the silk industry, where competition with France was fierce.

In July 1836, Parliament granted £1600 toward the foundation of the National School of Design in London. By 1843 there were eight other schools receiving grant support; these included Spitalfields, York, Nottingham, Sheffield, Coventry, Birmingham and Newcastle. There is little evidence that Macclesfield campaigned actively for government resources until the late 1840s and the town appears initially to have been content with the activities of the Useful Knowledge Society.

At the first annual meeting of the Useful Knowledge Society in 1836 a membership of 16 was reported. By the following year this had risen to 60 with 44 attending the drawing classes. By 1842 the Society was installed in premises on Dog Lane (now Stanley Street). In the following year Mr Gordon, the secretary, reported that "among the members instructed by the Society in the eight years of its operation eleven were holding responsible jobs, of which two were designers for silk houses".

The annual report of 1845 records that the Society had several of its students studying at the Manchester School of Design. By 1847 at least two students had gone on to study in London. William Corns had been supported by Edward John, (later Lord) Stanley, to attend the Normal School of Design in London. Joseph Lynch, having first studied design at Manchester, was maintained by Mr Davenport, a prominent member of the Society, whilst studying in London. Others were to follow later in the century. The Useful Knowledge Society had outgrown its premises by 1847 and required either more room or less students. It was proposed that the Society might purchase the large Sunday School from the Trustees for £7,000. However, for legal or other reasons, this did not materialise. Fundraising activities were held and the former parsonage building on Park Green was purchased by the Society.

John Brocklehurst MP, President of the Society, continued to work towards achieving Government funding to support a School of Design in Macclesfield. At the annual meeting in 1850 he was reported as stating that "as there existed 14 or 15 Government schools in manufacturing towns, Macclesfield thought itself entitled to one equal with the others". He also reported that "in 1850 Parliament had raised the sum voted to support these schools from £10,000 to

City and Guilds prize awarded to William Rothwell 1906

Owen Jones Competiton bronze medal awarded to William B Wright 1910

Macclesfield School of Art

David Jones, who trained as a designer at BWA, demonstrating handloom weaving to vistitors at Paradise Mill Museum 1988

'Hare & Hound' Jacquard woven silk designed by a student at Macclesfield School of Art c1920

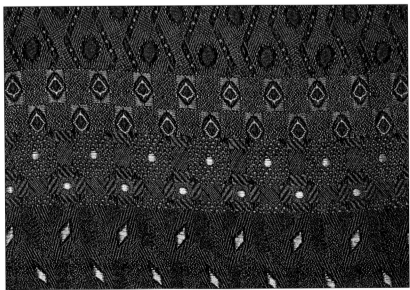

Designs 1932-3 by Leslie Robinson, who attended Macclesfield School of Art

James Ward (Headmaster 1888-1907)

£14,500, but that an essential condition of this support was that the School of Design should be an entirely separate and distinct institution". In 1852 the School of Art was established as a separate institution in accommodation that had been added above the Useful Knowledge Society premises in Park Green. The first headmaster was George Stewart 1851-64. He was followed by James Ford, 1864-79. During the early 1870s the accommodation in Park Green was considered inadequate by the government inspectors and in 1874 it was determined that a new school should be built. The Macclesfield Corporation granted a site on Old Park Lane, adjacent to the library and reading room. In February 1877 plans were drawn up by Alfred Stephens, a local architect, and were approved by the Science and Art Department in South Kensington.

Ford claims that he filled the Macclesfield factories with designers while on his arrival "There was hardly a designer who had been taught by the school". While other evidence does not support this it is clear that the number of designers attending increased under Ford. He had done much to make the work of the school more relevant to the practical needs of the industry although this had threatened examination results and, following a disagreement with the committee, Ford resigned. He established the new School of Art and Design in Albert Building, Waters Green, but it did not prosper and, in 1881 he emigrated to South Africa and became Head of the New Colonial School of Art in Cape Town.

Walter Scott succeeded Ford and during his term of office, from 1879 to 1888, the school became firmly established with enviable results in the national examinations and competitions. In design the school was rated as fifth in the country for several years and first in 1882 and 1883. Despite these results Scott resigned under unhappy circumstances and became Head of the Norwich School of Art.

By 1888, when James Ward was appointed, Macclesfield School of Art was rated as one of the leading art schools in the country with a strong emphasis on design. During his period the success in examinations and competitions continued and Ward's personal reputation as an author of textbooks on design served to enhance further the school's reputation. A native of Belfast, he left Macclesfield in 1907 to become Principal of The Royal Metropolitan School of Art, Dublin. Ward was succeeded by his former pupil of nine years, Thomas Cartwright, who had studied at The Royal College of Art and in Paris and Lyon with a travelling scholarship.

An inspection by His Majesty's Inspectors in 1909 found the school well organised and the teaching suited to the needs of students. The work of the school was principally orientated towards industrial study for silk designers and weavers.

Cartwright's annual report for 1922 recorded in the Textile Mercury of 27 January 1923 stated that "while the work done by the textile students is excellent in quality the number of students gets less every year". In August that year the same publication recording the examination results for Macclesfield states - "high though Macclesfield School of Art has ranked over the schools of the country which specialised in the production of industrial designs its results this year surpass any previously recorded in its history".

Four years later further recognition was given to the school in the Textile Journal of January 1927 "In education facilities Macclesfield designers have much to be thankful for; the schools of Art and Technology have always been open to them and many of the teachers, designers and cloth experts in all parts of the country and in America have to thank their old school, Art Masters and the technical instructors for their excellent training".

Technical training had been carried out alongside training in art and design. In the years leading up to and following the Cobden Treaty, the local manufacturers expressed the desire to improve both art and technical training. In 1860 the Useful Knowledge Society restructured its courses introducing instruction in 'silk manufacture and design', advanced arithmetic, natural philosophy and chemistry.

In the early 1880s a view was expressed that the lack of technical education was one of the reasons for the decline of the Macclesfield Silk Industry. A Technical Education Sub Committee of the Chamber of Commerce was formed in October 1882 but it was not until October 1886 that the Technical School finally opened in the Useful Knowledge Society premises on Park Green. The syllabus included throwing, weaving, theory and practice of weaving, pattern designing and construction of power and handlooms.

Under the Headship of Ward closer links were established between the School of Art and the Technical School. It was not until 1936 that the schools came under one principal, Mr Bonnard, who had succeeded Cartwright as Head of the School of Art in 1927. However, the school was never again to enjoy the reputation it had held in the late 19th and first quarter of the 20th century. Today, although the building continues to be used for further and vocational education as part of Macclesfield College, it no longer trains designers and technicians for the silk industry. The teaching of weaving ceased in 1957, although textile designers continued to attend classes at the Art School into the 1970s.

Thomas Cartwright (Headmaster 1907-1927)

Designers

It is clear that throughout their history Macclesfield textile manufacturers used local independent designers, employed 'in house' designers and purchased designs from elsewhere in Britain and Europe. Many firms subscribed to pattern services, for example Brocklehursts bought services from France, Switzerland and America. This was to keep abreast of contemporary design trends and to act as a creative stimulus for the 'in house' designers.

The earliest reference to designers in the town appears in the 1841 census; father and son John and William Corns, are both listed as designers in Sutton. The latter attended the Useful Knowledge Society drawing classes in the 1840s and was offered a place at the London School of Design. He later became a textile manufacturer and by 1871 he was employing 400 people.

Between 1851 and 1873, seventy seven textile designers had received training at the School of Art. However, it is not clear how many of these were employed by silk manufacturers in the town. In 1886 John Godwin, designer, was able to inform the Royal Commission on the Depression of Trade and Industry, that "while in 1874/5, two years after he had moved to the town, there had been only 30 designers in Macclesfield employed by just 6 firms, by 1886 there were 100 employed by 18 firms'.

Godwin does not make the distinction between independent designers and 'in house' designers but it would imply that many were being employed directly by the silk manufacturers since Slater's Directory for 1887/88 lists only 6 independent designers: Herbert Ashton, John Godwin, Peter Hollinshead, Gustave Hare, John Sherwood and Alexander Young.

The firm of John Godwin is recorded at Athey Street Mill. This firm had been established in Manchester in the 1820s and had moved to Macclesfield in 1873. The pattern books (dated from the 1840s to the early 1900s) of this independent design firm survive in the Museum's collections. John Godwin and Sons worked for textile manufacturers throughout the country and the pattern books include designs for woven linen damasks and printed cottons in addition to the silk design for items such as figured bandannas and ladies Jacquard woven scarves of the 1870s.

The minutes of the Macclesfield Silk Manufacturers Society, a weavers co-operative, records paying bills for design to Sherwood and P Hollinshead in 1889. The following year the minutes record that J Donaghue is authorised as a designer. Although his name does not appear in Slater's Directory he does appear in the list of National Prize Winners in the annual reports of the Art School. By 1917 the minutes of the Macclesfield Textile Manufacturers Society refer to "Mr Cundiff, Head Designer" suggesting that by this stage

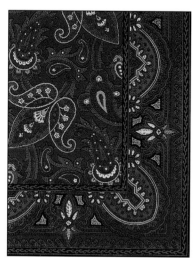

James Walmsley - Block print designer 1920s

Block printed quarter design

the firm had more than one designer employed in house. Even when the firms employed their own large design team it was common to purchase other designs. Harold W Whiston, despite employing a substantial design team at the Langley Printworks, states that "To maintain novelty in style and colouring, I engaged the finest designers in Paris, Lyon, Mulhouse, Zurich and Vienna and with them the necessary block makers were engaged all over Europe".

In 1885, in his report on the English Silk Industry written for the Royal Commission on Technical Instruction, Thomas Wardle lamented that Macclesfield manufacturers preferred to use French designs, rather than make use of the talents of local designers trained by the School of Art. This is surprising since many of the manufacturers in the town had trained at the School of Art. However, it would appear that while local designers did work in the industry many firms preferred to copy foreign designs; hence many designers, trained at the School of Art, sought employment in silk and other textile industries outside Macclesfield. Frank Warner was a regular visitor to Macclesfield and clearly valued the designers trained at Macclesfield School of Art. He was to offer two Macclesfield trained designers employment in London and Braintree. The first was Bertrand Whitaker who was a student at the Macclesfield School of Art in 1897 and elected as an Associate in 1908, the year in which he joined Warners. He was followed by Herbert Woodman who joined Warners as a designer in 1920 and rose to become a director.

Fred Cope had also trained at the Macclesfield School of Art and in 1908 was elected an Associate. In the period 1898 to 1913 he had achieved numerous prizes in the National Design Competitions. He joined Cartwright and Sheldon, who were established in 1912, and became head designer. He was highly valued by the firm and in 1912 was the highest paid member of staff earning £2.10s (£2.50) per week, possibly to avoid his defection to another company.

In 1947 Clifford Brown joined Cartwright & Sheldon; at that time there were two other designers, Harry Worsley and Leslie Robinson working under Fred Cope. Clifford Brown had trained at the Macclesfield School of Art and taught there prior to the closure of the weaving and design courses. When Cartwright & Sheldon ceased trading in 1982 he joined James Arnold & Company as design manager.

Probably the best known designer to have worked at James Arnold was Arthur Oldfield, who joined the firm prior to the First World War. An Associate of Macclesfield School of Art and winner of numerous national prizes he had attended the Royal College of Art. The Board of Education South

Bill Hine designer of 'The Mayflower' 1969

'The Mayflower', BWA woven silk picture

Kensington purchased from him a design for a woven silk hanging for circulation to the different schools of art throughout Britain. His work also appeard in 'The Studio' and 'Der Moderne Stil'

J & T Brocklehurst & Sons Ltd., as the largest silk manufacturer in the town, probably employed the largest design team. In 1928, the year before its amalgamation to become Brocklehurst Whiston Amalgamated, William Hine, aged 15, joined the staff to take up a five year apprenticeship as a Jacquard designer, under Richard Charles Riseley, the Head Designer. The apprenticeship involved studying for the City and Guilds examinations and he attended Macclesfield School of Art on three nights per week, Mondays and Fridays for City and Guilds textiles and one other night for drawing. Bill Hine's grandfather, mother and uncle were also designers, the latter working for Godwins producing designs for the cotton trade. By the late 1970s, when he retired, he had risen to the position of Head Designer with Brocklehurst Fabrics Limited. According to David Jones, who joined the Design Department in 1945 when Jim Norris was head designer, the design studio at Hurdsfield Mill on Fence Avenue was mainly devoted to woven designs. With the exception of scarf designs undertaken by Sidney Barlow, all print design was undertaken at Langley Print Works.

In recent years the number of designers employed have declined with the industry. It has not been possible to mention all the designers employed by Macclesfield firms but the aim has been to include a selection where their work appears in the pattern books of the collections studied.

The tradition of woven and printed designs in Macclesfield is currently being continued by Michael Bateson and Eric Hockenhull, the designers employed by Adamley Textiles, the only firm still producing both woven and printed designs for silk textiles. Other firms continue to employ in-house and freelance designers for Jacquard designs mainly produced in polyester. Since Brocklehurst Fabrics and James Arnold & Company closed in 1991 and 1993 respectively, Mottersheads continue to weave Jacquard fabrics mainly in polyester for the club tie market and Spurcroft, established in 1981, produces Jacquard woven silk and polyester fabrics designed by John Collins and Gareth Emblin for neckwear.

Although design is a profession dominated by men it is not a totally male preserve. Following the opening of the new School of Art building on old Park Lane in 1879, it was reported that the ladies' classes more than doubled. However, the Committee wished to ask in connection with the increase "why the Macclesfield Silk trade, so largely engaged in marketing fabrics for ladies use, has not attempted to employ female labour in its designing departments. The country has its female porcelain painters, its female art embroidery workers, its female artists at the Lambeth pottery works, but your committee know of no female silk designers in Macclesfield, and would ask, why not?".

Between 1885 and 1915 a number of women appear in the prizes of the National Competitions however, with only minor exceptions, the awards are either for fine art or art embroidery designs. The latter may have had some commercial relevance since J O Nicholson, the Secretary of the School of Art, had established the School of Embroidery in his Mill in 1882 to train working girls in the skills of art embroidery for commercial production.

Hewetson design studio 1950s

Evidence of women playing a significant role in the design departments is slim until the second quarter of the twentieth century, although it would appear from oral history interviews that the mother of Bill Hine, a textile designer born in 1913, was a designer. In 1947 all five prizes in the Textile Institute Competition for Textile Design Printed Fabrics Class I, Designs for dress material, were awarded to female designers at Brocklehurst Whiston Amalgamated. All five would have at that time been working at Langley under the head of print design, Miss Bentley.

Female Jacquard designers are few in number, although many women were employed as 'dotters' to complete the ground areas of the drafts. Carolyn Cook trained at Brocklehursts and is now a design manager in Congleton. Susan Dean trained in Galashiels and was employed by James Arnold & Company, while Karen Emblin has worked as a freelance Jacquard designer in the town.

Sue Magee (nee Hyland) heads a print design team at Barracks Fabrics. Sue joined the firm in 1976 after attending Macclesfield School of Art where she studied History of Art and Textile Design. The major part of the work of Barracks studio is in developing and adapting customers' ideas or designs for printing. Occasionally speculative designs are undertaken but the firm is essentially a commission printer producing the designs for internationally known designers of fashion and furnishings.

Today little speculative work is done by any of the textile firms in the town whether as printers or weavers. The firms are largely engaged in realising the designs of their customers which are as far afield as America.

The designs of the past continue to be used by customers who draw from the archives held by local manufacturers to develop contemporary collections in fashion and furnishings. Hence the work of Macclesfield designers of the past might be found in the fashion and furnishing collections of the 1990s.

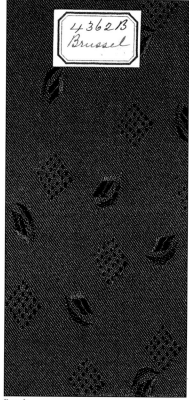

Brussels

Sarsenet

Barathea

Damask

Satin

Pongee

Fibres and Fabrics

Joseph Marie Jacquard (1752-1834)

The Macclesfield textile industry was predominantly silk but throughout its history a wide range of other fibres and fabrics have been produced. In the 16th century there is evidence of a fulling mill at Sutton suggesting a small scale woollen industry in the vicinity. Cotton was spun in the town alongside silk in the late 18th and early 19th centuries but this had largely died out by the 1820s and became concentrated in the mills in the northern area of East Cheshire, in towns and villages such as Bollington, Styal and Disley. Silk had been associated with Macclesfield since the 16th century when it was used with mohair to produce worked buttons and button twist. Low quality silk and silk waste was also used to produce narrow fabrics like hat bands, ferrets and galloons. The silk was originally thrown and twisted by hand in the small low buildings or shelters known as 'shades'. It was the introduction of powered throwing technology in the mid 18th century which resulted in the town building the first of over 120 mills which were essentially used for yarn processing. Weaving of narrow fabrics continued alongside the powered throwing industry and by the end of the 18th century broad loom weaving had become established on a small scale and by the 1840s shaft, swivel and Jacquard looms were in use in the production of broad silk fabrics. It is likely that the first Jacquard machine was in use by the 1820s. In the price list of 1840 reference is made to prices for work produced on up to 32 shaft looms and 100, 200, 400 and 600 Jacquard machines. The price for the loom rent which weavers paid to masters is also quoted in the price list of 1840:- Weavers paid 2s.0d (£0.10) for rent of a shaft loom and 4s.0d (£0.20) for rent of a Jacquard machine.

Although the earliest reference to a Jacquard loom in the town was in the 1820s, it would appear that the full potential of Jacquard weaving in Macclesfield had not been realised by the 1840s. J Brocklehurst, speaking to the Useful Knowledge Society in 1850, is reported as stating that 'the introduction of the Jacquard loom at that time had given a vast impetus to weaving and he saw that in its application to the silk industry had great potential for Macclesfield'. It could be interpreted from this that the Jacquard machines had seen little use in the industry of Macclesfield at that time. Whether this is true or not is difficult to establish from the limited number of pattern books which have survived from that date. After 1850 the number of Jacquard patterns certainly increases in the pattern books and Jacquard designs predominate during the 1860s and 1870s.

Spun silk seems to have been introduced in the 19th century. Crozier, writing in 1947, claims that short staple spinning was undertaken by

Brocklehursts in the 1820s and long staple spinning was introduced in the 1840s when they were given the rights to use the 'patent long spun' process developed by Gibson and Campbell of Glasgow, a concession granted as a result of Brocklehursts solving their liquidity problems. Brocklehursts were also engaged in weaving Tussah silk. William Coare Brocklehurst took a great interest in the cultivation of Tussah silk in India on which he worked with Sir Thomas Wardle of Leek. Wardle had developed techniques for dyeing Tussah silk which he had first exhibited in 1873 at the International Exhibition in South Kensington. James Kershaw had 100 looms engaged on weaving Tussah silk for seaside wear in the 1870s. Examples of Tussah fabrics can be seen in the Brocklehurst pattern books of the late 19th century and it was clearly being produced by others in the town in 1895 when the Duchess of Teck visited.

In the 20th century the fabric for which Macclesfield is perhaps best known is spun crepe silk. This had a spun silk warp and a thrown silk weft. It was durable, colourfast with excellent washing properties and soft to handle. It was produced from the 1920s to the 1940s in plain colours and stripes, the latter being known as 'Macclesfield Stripe'. It was popular for summer dresses, blouses and sportswear and was marketed actively in the 1930s alongside the new man-made fibres.

Although there is substantial evidence for many experiments in the production of artificial fibres from the 1850s and Joseph (later Sir Joseph) Swan exhibited artificial silk yarn and goods at the Inventions Exhibition in 1885, it is Chardonnet who is credited as the father of man-made textile fibres. Count Hilaire de Chardonnet was born in Besançon, France, in 1840. Early in his career he worked with Louis Pasteur who in 1865 had been recruited by the French government to examine the cause of the disease which was threatening the silk worm population of France and thus the health of the French silk industry. Pasteur was engaged on the project for two years and successfully identified the malady known as 'Pebrine'. This gave Chardonnet the opportunity to observe silk worms over a long period and may have aroused his interest in creating a fibre to simulate silk. Indeed Chardonnet's early experiments had used mulberry leaves, the food of silk worms, as a source of cellulose in the nitro-cellulose process. However, this was later abandoned in favour of cotton and similar substances. Chardonnet patented his process in the winter of 1884/5 and in 1889 he exhibited the results of his work at a Paris Exhibition. Thomas Wardle had been a member of the jury at the exhibition and in a lecture to the Royal Society of Arts in 1891 said that "at the time the artificial silk did not arouse much interest" but two years later it seems to have

Hilaire le Comte de Chardonnet (1840-1924)

Bemberg Advertisement 1930s

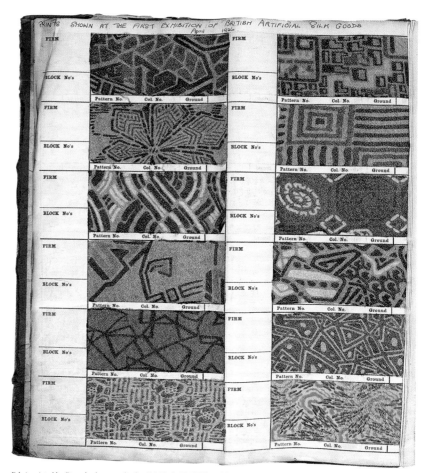

Fabric printed by Barracks shown at the first British Artificial Silk Exhibition 1926

been in commercial production and Wardle had samples to display at his lecture.

Chardonnet was awarded the Grand Prix and made a Knight of the Legion of Honour. His work attracted the interest of capitalists and the first factory was built at Besançon. By 1891 two further factories had been built in quick succession, one established in Tubize, Belgium, by the directors of Wardle and Davenport of Leek.

As leaders in the silk industry it is improbable that artificial silk did not attract the attention of the Macclesfield manufacturers. Throughout its history Brocklehursts had woven a number of mixed fibre fabrics and had produced various types of union cloth. It is possible that the 'silkette' exhibited by J & T Brocklehurst for the visit of the Duchess of Teck in 1895 was the first artificial silk to be manufactured in the town. It is described as "a new fabric suitable for ladies underwear". However, this may be just a description of a new pure silk fabric and the first date for weaving artificial silk may be that quoted by Wallace Ellison, Managing Director of Brocklehurst Whiston Amalgamated, who writing in 1945 states "the Company was the first in the town to weave rayon in 1900 and that the samples were at that time (1945) in the possession of Henry Bronnert and Company of Manchester". (Emile Bronnert, an Alsatian chemist, had also been engaged in developing the nitro-cellulose process for the production of man-made fibres).

Harold Whiston had begun knitting and printing artificial silk in 1914/15 and had employed Chardonnet, then aged 75, in 1915/16, to advise on the printing process. Writing in 1945 Whiston recalls that he received "much technical help from him in dyeing, printing and finishing these alternative materials".

By the 1920s artificial silk fabrics were being woven and printed alongside silk at most manufacturers. In 1926, two years after they were established, Barracks Fabrics exhibited samples of printed rayons at the first British Artificial Silk Exhibition in London. Rayon had been adopted by the American manufacturers as generic term for the man-made fibres in 1924. Man-made textile fibres which were developed in the late 19th and early 20th centuries fall into four major categories: (1) nitro-celloluse or Chardonnet rayon, (2) viscose rayons, (3) cuprammonium rayon, (4) cellulose acetate. All are based on cellulose derived mainly from cotton. The fibre which was reputed to most closely resemble the properties of silk was the cuprammonium rayon which was woven in Macclesfield under the trade name of Bemberg. It was also used extensively in the hosiery business.

Printed by Barracks for the Imperial Chemical Co. 1932-33

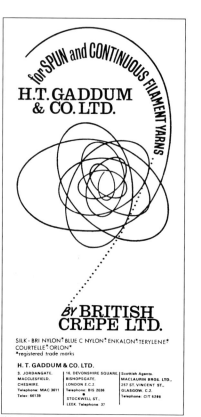

for SPUN and CONTINUOUS FILAMENT YARNS.

H.T. GADDUM & CO. LTD.

BY **BRITISH CREPE LTD.**

SILK · BRI NYLON* BLUE C NYLON* ENKALON* TERYLENE*
COURTELLE* ORLON*
*registered trade marks

H. T. GADDUM & CO. LTD.

| 3, JORDANGATE, MACCLESFIELD, CHESHIRE. Telephone: MAC 3611 Telex: 66139 | 16, DEVONSHIRE SQUARE, BISHOPSGATE, LONDON E.C.2. Telephone: BIS 2036 ● STOCKWELL ST., LEEK. Telephone: 37 | Scottish Agents: MACLAURIN BROS. LTD., 257, ST. VINCENT ST., GLASGOW. C.2. Telephone: CIT 6298 |

Skinners Directory 1967

The second generation of man-made fibres were known as synthetics and were based on polymers, the first of these being nylon. Nylon was first made in the laboratories of Du Pont de Nemours of America. Research began in 1928 by studying natural materials like rubber, cellulose and silk. Work concentrated on a particular group of polymers known as the polymides and after 10 years of exhaustive research the new fibre known as Nylon was announced to the public in October 1938. Commercial production followed the next year. The first factory was established in England by British Nylon Spinners in January 1941 and was followed by a second in December 1942 with all the production of the two factories used for war purposes.

The silk manufacturers in Macclesfield were well placed to work with the chemical manufacturers who were developing and experimenting with new fibres. The skills of the industry in weaving, dyeing and printing were employed to test the new fibres. Brocklehursts was one of the first to weave nylon and oral history interviews confirm that there were early technical problems with static electricity causing the warp to spark as it passed through the reed and the weft to fly and stick to everything. Nylon was used for parachute fabric towards the end of the Second World War and was soon developed for other uses. Terylene, a polyester fibre, invented by The Calico Printers Association and later developed by ICI made a significant impact on the men's neckwear trade. Today, Terylene is used extensively on its own for the production of tie fabric and mixed with other fabrics for a wide range of products. Crimplene, a texturised polyester fibre, was developed in Macclesfield by Mario Nava, an Italian who moved to Macclesfield in 1934 and established Cheslene and Crepes Limited. He was interned in 1940 but released the same year and resumed working for Cheslene and Crepes in 1941. Working with Scraggs, the Macclesfield machinery manufacturer, Nava developed and patented Crimplene but sold the rights to ICI who later took over Cheslene and Crepes. Today Mowbrays continue to process and texturise synthetic yarns for use in weaving, knitting and lace industries in Britain and overseas.

Dyeing and Printing

The dyeing industry in Macclesfield developed in tandem with the silk industry. As the silk industry expanded dyeworks became more complex. By the mid 1800s there were about 20 dyers in the town; in addition some mills had their own dyehouses. Most firms adapted to dyeing of man-made fibres alongside silk as technology developed, but today only one dyeworks, Massie and sons remains in business in Macclesfield with two firms having their own dye sections.

Several firms have been associated with printing; the most significant was founded in Langley just outside Macclesfield, about 1820, by William Smith. The earliest products were the hand tying and dyeing of silk and printing with wax resists; these pieces were then dyed in indigo. Other processes which were developed at Langley in the 19th and 20th century and no longer commonly used are:- plate printing using copper plates (which were requisitioned during the First World War, making the revival of this technique almost impossible), resist and pad printing – a simple and cheap system used for the large Eastern market towards the end of the 19th century, and rayonee printing which ceased in the 1930s.

The Langley Printing Company passed from William Smith and his son John to William Whiston then his son Harold and in 1929 amalgamated with J & T Brocklehurst to form a formidable partnership. A large collection of the print pattern books now forms part of the Brocklehurst Whiston Archive and shows examples of many of the techniques employed.

The firm acquired handblocks from a number of prominent firms and amassed the largest collection of hand blocks in Europe, with the purchase in 1895 of blocks from Baker, Tucker & Company, and followed by the Persian and Kashmir blocks from the Swaisland Printing Company alongside other smaller collections. The firm had a block engraving shop and made many of its own blocks.

Harold Whiston experimented using a German synthetic dye which proved very successful. Langley specialised in printing using the real madder process and many examples exist in the pattern books showing the special effect in the colour which the madder produces.

In Harold Whiston's opinion, his most important innovation was "the replacing of the traditional mitred corners for handkerchiefs and mufflers by the more perfect corners produced by using quarto blocks" (4 blocks to a square).

For many years the industry concentrated on the production of menswear but eventually expanded into the ladies' market. Hand block printing upon silk of traditional foulards was supplemented by similar effects on man-made fibres.

Block engraving Langley 1948

Examining a corner block Langley 1948

W Boothby block printing a foulard pattern

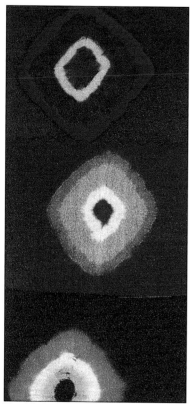

Tie and dye design for Coles 1932-33

The pattern books contain examples of plate printing from the 1850s through to the 1880s with many of the designs bearing a date of registration. The block printing allover designs date from the 1850s through to the 1950s thus showing 100 years production.

Hand screen printing was introduced at Langley and at the Barracks Printing Company in the 1920s as a cheaper and quicker alternative to hand block printing. Hand screen printing is retained for very short run high quality work and sampling. Barracks was the first to introduce to England photographic techniques for engraving screens. Improvements in photo-engraving has meant a raising of print standards. The introduction of machine printing in 1956 saw the use of hand blocks gradually dying out.

The Barracks Archive does not contain examples of the earliest production which included stencil printing, but from 1926 it gives details of designs, customers and the length of time a design was in production.

Apart from hand and screen printing the pattern books show examples of discharge and metallic printing and the heat cloque process. Barracks has always been innovative and generally prints short runs for the upper end of the market. Barracks print for a number of well known customers, including Libertys, but in the past has also printed scarves and handkerchiefs for Macclesfield firms such as Edmund Lomas, Joseph Dunkerley and Cartwright & Sheldon who had making-up departments. The range of designs are predominantly for fashion fabrics with some furnishings. As well as silk, the firm printed, and still does print, on a variety of materials including cotton, wool, and man-made fibres, concentrating on fairly short runs.

Today the firm are commission printers printing in acid, pigment, reactive and vat dyestuffs on widths up to 152cm in 20 colours. Finishing processes include crease resist, flame retardent, soil resist, sandwashed, water repellent, chintz and polish finishes.

Adamley Textiles began in 1965 as a hand block printing business. Today the firm dyes its own fabric and yarns and has a substantial hand screen printing department.

Tie and dye - BWA Langley 1948

Copper plate print designs registered by William Whiston & Son 1863–65

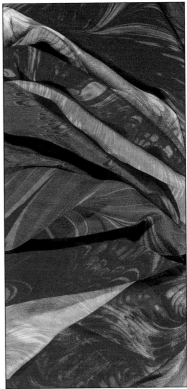

Rayonee printing used 'an intensely foul smelling animal product' 1920s

Screen printing 1948

Customers

Little is known about the distribution of Macclesfield products in the early 19th century, although links with London were established through the supplying of organzine to the Spitalfields weavers and through the button merchants of the 17th and 18th centuries. The chapmen on horseback took Macclesfield products well beyond the local environs.

Mary Crozier refers to ledgers dating to the 1750s in her history of the Brocklehurst firm. It would appear that the main customers were the London and Manchester export and home trade houses like Samuel Greg & Co., S & W Hibbert and Entwistles. The firm's direct foreign trade was to Jacob David Levy, Amsterdam, John Thomson, New York and Kruger & Rissenkampff, Moscow. There also appears to have been a substantial Scottish business.

In 1818 the report on the Committee on Petitions for Silk Ribbon Weavers stated that "the windows here in London used to have printed papers upon their bandannas stating them to be of Macclesfield manufacture".

In the last quarter of the 19th century entries in the local paper, the Macclesfield Courier and Herald, reported the importance of the Admiralty order for black silk. Competition by firms for the Navy contract were much sought after and J & T Brocklehurst and J Birchenough in particular obtained large orders.

At the same time the "Rangoon trade" was very extensive. Harold Whiston in his book "Langley" states that for 20 years (1875-1895) the firm averaged an output for the Rangoon market of 1000 pieces per day of (8)s of figured woven silks. The printing was simple, in a variety of fine styles. As well as benefiting the Langley Print Works, the volume of woven cloth required meant large orders for other firms, in particular J & T Brocklehurst and for Thomas Crew who undertook the finishing.

The main outlet for products were the large warehouses in London, Manchester and Glasgow. Firms often had a London office or alternatively employed representatives and agents. Overseas agents were established in New York, Paris and other European cities.

The Minutes of the Macclesfield Silk Manufacturing Society record the appointment of new representatives in Paris and New York in 1894, and in 1916 an agency was established in Spain. In 1905 the manager was directed by his Board to visit London once per month. The Society was unique in that its major outlet was through the Co-operative Wholesale Society although there is evidence that the firm also dealt directly with potential customers. The agents, representatives and regular visits by the firm's staff, meant an exchange of ideas and a feel for current trends in fashion.

The 'Silk Pretty' - *Courtesy of HMS Warrior*

Firms advertised their products by exhibiting at national and international exhibitions held in the major cities abroad and principal towns in the UK. As well as displaying products some manufacturers took looms to the exhibitions and demonstrated weaving. This idea had been introduced by Thomas Stevens of Coventry who wove "The Royal Mail Coach" at the York Exhibition of 1879. The awarding of gold medals and diplomas added to a firm's prestige.

Although some lists of customers exist and the Brocklehurst Whiston Amalgamated and Barracks books have the customer's name inscribed next to the design, in many instances codes and initials are used, making the interpretation of customers difficult.

Wholesalers who figure prominently in a number of firms' books include Aldwinckle, Holliday and Brown, Churchill and Mitchelson. J & T Brocklehurst worked with Sir Arthur Liberty from the latter's early days.

The Barracks Printing Co specialised in short runs of quality goods, printing for many well known companies such as Jacqmar, Ascher, Marks & Spencer, Liberty, Cresta Silks and Debenhams. For a period the majority of the trade was with Berne Silks.

Barracks also undertook printing for a number of local firms who had making up businesses producing printed scarves and handkerchiefs. These included Cartwright and Sheldon, Edmund Lomas, Halle's, Joseph Dunkerley and The Standard Manufacturing Co. Today Barracks is part of the Courtauld Group and still specialises in shorter runs of high quality for both fashion and furnishing outlets.

The American tie manufacturers account for 60% of Adamley Textiles trade. The other 40% is to the home trade who in turn export the finished product all over the world. The hemming business supplies handkerchiefs to the home market and overseas to Japan, Australia and New Zealand.

Other firms in Macclesfield engaged in the club tie trade supply the corporate wear suppliers at home and abroad, with some direct sales to individual organisations.

J & T Brocklehurst woven samples c1890

Printed at Langley for Welch Margetson c1910

Printed by Barracks for Cresta Silks 1935

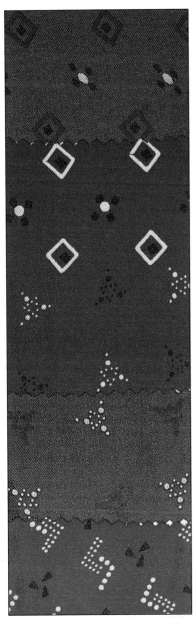

'neats' printed at Langley for Holiday and Brown 1945–49

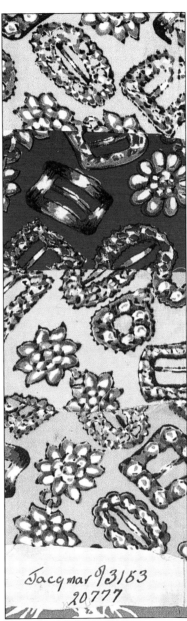

Jacqmar 93163
20777

Printed at Barracks for Jacqmar 1945–49

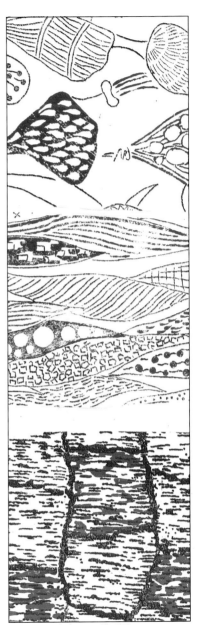

Printed at Barracks for Berne Silks 1947

43

Crepe Washing Frock

The yoke bodice is softly gathered and the skirt has box pleats ; braid belt to match with stitched crepon bands. In white, blue, pink, natural, yellow, turquoise, green and lilac. Sizes 40, 42, 44 and 45.

78/6

Sizes 46 and 48, **5/-** extra.

(Sent on approval)

DEBENHAM & FREEBODY

LONDON, W.1

1930s Advertisement

Printed by Barracks 1957-58 'Music' 72" skirt panel in red, blue, lime and black

Design for Edmund Lomas 1957-8

Design for Haslams in black and White

Cartwright & Sheldon 36" Scarf Design

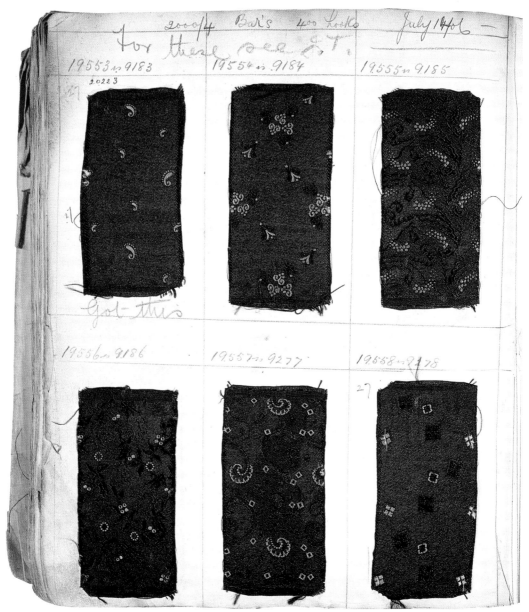

The Macclesfield Silk Manufacturing Society supplied to Co-operative societies: tie samples from 1906

Bianchini Ferrier design printed by Barracks 1954

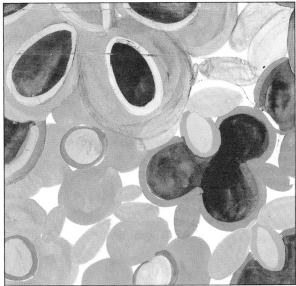

Liberty design printed by Barracks 1967

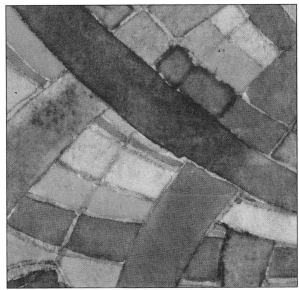

"Fontella:" Berne Silks design printed by Barracks 1967

Menswear

In the early years of the 19th century, the main product for which Macclesfield manufacturers were famous was the bandanna handkerchief, woven in the grey state. Advances in technology soon meant that figure work, using swivel looms, could be used for the production of different types of handkerchief such as Romols and Barcelonas.

The standard price list of 1840 showed the range of menswear extended to swivel and satin scarves, cravats, waistcoating and various types of bandanna - Barcelonas, Brussels and stripes varying in width from 28" to 36". Prices in 1849 are listed as:- new line grey bandannas - 7 squares to the cut, 26" - 36" width from 1s.4$\frac{1}{2}$d (£0.06). per cut to 3s.1$\frac{1}{2}$d (£0.15) for the best quality. Pongees 10 squares to the cut 26" @ 2s.9d (£0.14) to 3s.11d (£0.20) for 30". Satin scarves - 4 threads 14" @ 6d (£0.02.5) per yard, 10 threads 14" @ 10$\frac{1}{2}$d (£0.04) per yard

Other cloths included boys checked Brussels, black, coloured or stripe, military and crepe handkerchiefs. At the Great Exhibition in 1851, J & T Brocklehurst exhibited a range of products including gentlemen's black, coloured, plain and figured handkerchiefs, Levantines, serges, vestings and sarsnets. Henry and Thomas Wardle and Critchley and Brinsley displayed gentlemen's cravats and boys' neck-handkerchiefs. In the 1870s J O Nicholson exhibited in Paris and won a medal for the design and manufacture of scarves and silk handkerchiefs. From the 1880s and into the 20th century, the Admiralty contract for black handkerchiefs, known as Black Order or Silk Prettys, played an important part in the financial stability of several Macclesfield firms including J Birchenough and J & T Brocklehurst. In 1883 Birchenough's was awarded a contract for 4,600 dozen and in 1904 'the largest ever order' to Macclesfield firms was for 160,000 handkerchiefs.

The Macclesfield Courier and Herald records that the Shirtmakers Union was founded in 1890 and the Cameron Shirt Factory, opened in 1894, was well known for the quality of its products. (A number of firms manufactured shirting up until the Second World War.)

The Duchess of Teck, as President of the Ladies Section of the Silk Association, promoted silk enthusiastically. In 1895 she visited Macclesfield and the local manufacturers displayed their products. We can see the range of goods then being produced as each firm exhibiting was listed with details of products.

Menswear shown by Josiah Smale featured gents' tie silks, gents' mufflers, handkerchiefs and printed foulards. J & T Brocklehurst showed tennis shirtings and black navy handkerchiefs, a large part of the firm's trade at this

Seamen wearing summer uniform with the Admiralty black silk square c1900 - *courtesy Royal Naval Museum*

time, whilst J Birchenough included silk mufflers, Colclough exhibited shepherd checks, spot twills, swivel handkerchiefs and tie cloths and gents' mufflers. James Kershaw exhibited handkerchiefs "in a hundred combinations" and mufflers - "gaudy and showy for country people" The most prominent manufacturers at the end of the century were producing rich silk cut ups, mufflers, scarves and vestings.

Contemporary newspaper comment stated that "Hitherto the work has been chiefly mufflers and handkerchiefs for gentlemen's wear but firms are now being stimulated to take a larger proportion of the dress silk trade".

After this time tie material began to take a larger share of the menswear market. The Factory Inspector's Report of 1904 recorded a decline in broad silk weaving, but a new industry in the production of ties, 28" squares for top quality ties alongside the 24" 'cut ups' for the cheaper product were much in evidence by the beginning of the 20th century. The cut ups were woven per cut of 7 either as checks or Jacquard, whilst 28" squares produced the "steel" for which Macclesfield became associated alongside the "neats". 24" handkerchiefs were still in demand with mufflers in a variety of widths, lengths and weaves. Cartwright & Sheldon, founded in 1912, were particularly well

Woven by J & T Brocklehurst c1850

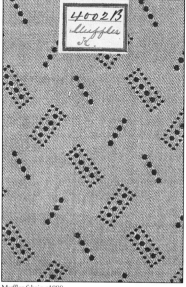

Muffler fabric c1890

Shirting fabric c1890

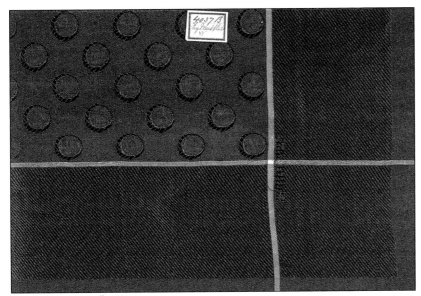

Corner of a figured satin muffler 1890s

Figured scarf fabric c1890 Woven by J & T Brocklehurst

Satin muffler fabric c1890

Coronation novelties by T H Hambleton 1937

known for the quality of their 28" handloom woven squares.

In the 1920s menswear products from Macclesfield firms still featured shirting, dressing gown material, foulards, handkerchiefs, squares and mufflers, but for the first time school, club and Regimental ties which became the main industry after the Second World War appeared. The Macclesfield longscarf was marketed at this time but was somewhat short lived, surviving for less than 20 years. Ties were woven in strips and not cut on the bias, producing a straight end, usually with the manufacturer's name woven along the bottom. The ties did not hang as well as conventional styles and so were never very popular. A number of firms produced ties of different qualities, for example, the Tootal "green" and "red" and the Brocklehurst gold tassel which had a tassel sewn into the tip; these were all produced as selling aids.

Whilst most firms manufactured a similar range of goods, particularly neckwear, there were firms who specialised, such as Oberland Silk Manufacturing Co, who produced hat linings and evening dress coat facings. Several firms wove Jewish prayer shawls.

The firm of Cartwright and Sheldon typified Macclesfield menswear production of the 1930s. As well as 28" squares the firm produced cut ups for ties, long scarves, vestings, dressing gown cloth, Jacquard mufflers and printed handkerchiefs.

After the Second World War firms were using man made fibres such as bemberg, terylene and rayon to produce ties for the expanding club tie market. Brocklehursts still printed and wove silk until their closure in 1991, as does Adamley Textiles today, mainly for the American market, but facing strong competition from Italy for the fashion trade.

There are nearly two hundred years of experience behind Brocklehurst Silk Yarns. The story of their progress is almost the history of silk production in England. Every era, every fashion since that time has placed reliance on Brocklehurst Yarns. During this period has been built up a fine reputation for quality. In these times of intensive competition, however, a high and traditional reputation for quality is not enough. That is why the production and marketing of Brocklehurst Yarns have recently been reorganised by scientific co-operation and grouping of plant. As a result of this, progressively controlled production and long-famous reputation for quality are now allied to the most modern conceptions of service. They are at your disposal. Why not use them?

BROCKLEHURST-WHISTON AMALGAMATED LIMITED HURDSFIELD MILLS, MACCLESFIELD London: Leith House, Gresham St., E.C.2 Agencies throughout the World

Agents : LEICESTER : W. H. Potter and Company, 29 York Road. GLASGOW : McLennan Blair & Co., 29 Montrose Street, Glasgow, C.I. *REPRESENTATIVES* : Mr. G. S. Hunt, Mr. H. Stonier (M.c. Royal Ex. Tues. & Fri.)

BROCKLEHURST
real silk yarns

Advertisement 1930s

Macclesfield longscarves 1920s–30s

Jacquard woven 'steel' tie design by John Barlow 1904

BWA Gold Tassel c1930

Jacquard woven design for vesting by John Barlow 1904

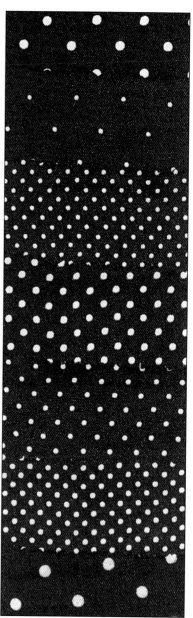

'Neat' tie design printed at Langley 1934–35

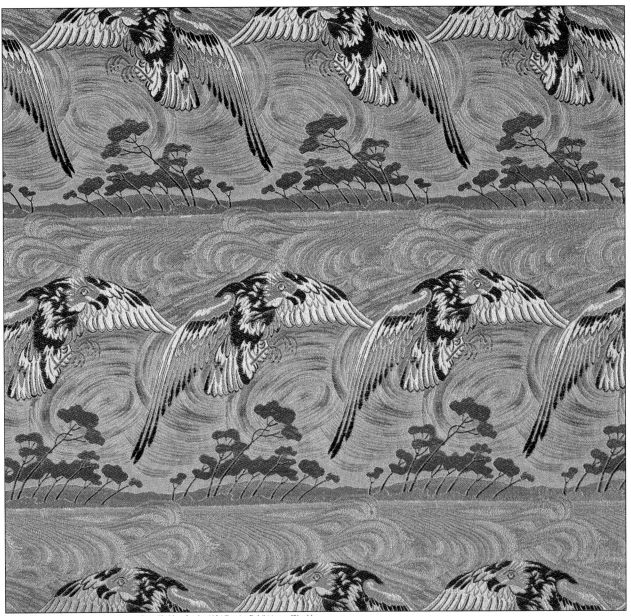

'Birds of Paradise' design woven by Cartwright & Sheldon for the 1924 Empire Exhibition at Wembley

Womenswear

Macclesfield is not associated with the production of quality fabrics for female dresses in the 18th century and it is difficult to establish clearly the precise scale or nature of production throughout this period as we are dependent on very few documentary sources and no surviving provenanced material. The earliest surviving pattern books attributed to Macclesfield are of the 1840s and show a range of figured broad silks mainly of a lightweight quality designed for handkerchief and bandannas. It is clear from the price list of 1840 that the greatest proportion of production was for handkerchiefs, bandannas, shawls and cut ups of various kinds, which are priced by 'the cut' or the dozen. There are however a number of items which are priced by the yard, these include Persians, mock sarsenets, sarsenets, barrettees or iris, velvet, striped velvet, Dutch velvet, Genoa, modes, armozine, figured gros and check dress. Twill satin and ducape shawls also appear in the lists. These are quoted from 35 to 72 inches in width and are priced by the dozen. For example for a satin shawl, 8 thread, 2,400 reed, 54" wide the weaver would receive £3.10s (£3.50) per dozen, while for a dozen 72" wide the weaver would be paid 5s.0d (£0.25) in 1840.

By 1851 it is evident from the material which Macclesfield companies exhibited at the Great Exhibition that a number of firms were manufacturing broad silks suitable for female dress. J & T Brocklehurst, the largest of the Macclesfield firms, exhibiting in class 13 "Silk and Velvet" showed a wide range of broad silks including velvets, satins, moire antiques, glace, gros de Naples (figured and plain), Levantines, serges, vestings, sarsenets and Persians. In addition to ribbons, hat furniture, ladies handkerchiefs, (coloured, plain and figured), shawls and gauze veils were exhibited.

Brinsley and Critchley & Co exhibited ladies foulard dresses, aprons and neckties. Henry and Thomas Wardle exhibited ladies handkerchiefs plain and checked, figured and chine, and ladies small silk shawls.

Designs and samples of cotton fabrics of the 1850s and 1860s appear in the sample books of J Godwin & Sons, designers. Although cotton was woven in the town it is not clear whether these designs were produced locally since Godwin's worked for a wide range of customers outside Macclesfield. Many of these designs are again for bandannas, but among these are a large number of designs for ladies scarves and cut ups.

In 1895 James Ward, headmaster of Macclesfield School of Art, mounted an exhibition in the school premises for the visit of the Duchess of Teck who was a great supporter of the English Silk Industry. Firms exhibited a wide range of products many being suitable for female dress including:- flowered chine dress silk warp printed by Whiston of Langley; white figure pongee for evening dress; rich white satin brocade for evening dress; printed and fringed shawls or evening wraps; rich stuffs in handsome dark mixtures for blouses; ladies Tussah dress cloths; a new fabric called 'silkette' for ladies underwear; special dress goods including white and black broche and black ottoman; ladies handkerchiefs; shepherd checks; spot twills; swivel handkerchiefs; figured brocades; matt and cream silk for blouses; fancy dress silks for dress trimmings; self colour surah for blouses; rich black dress silks; gros grains (or foundation silks) for dress linings; figured silks for blouses and trimmings; ivory figured and other figured silks for blouses; made up blouses in the newest patterns and styles; very pretty short handkerchiefs; cut ups for the French, American and English market; handkerchiefs in cream with primrose, fuchsia and lily patterns to be worn as headdresses by ladies of Spain and Algeria, others with plain centres and broad figured borders; check twills for dresses and blouses; bright Madras stripe in several colours used for lining capes etc; shot surahs and washing silks; piece silks for dresses; rich satins and blouse silks; check surahs for dress and blouses; sashes with plain and fancy fringes; ladies scarves; hat trimmings; figured and plain dress silks; plain china; printed foulards; Madras check surahs; ladies mufflers etc; silk for ties and blouses, and shot squares; made up blouses in gold and ivory with chine effect; silk tartans in various designs for the Scottish trade; black and white checks; figured goods; rich figured sashes and rich silks for dresses; trimmings for decorative purposes. Clearly by 1895 a significant part of Macclesfield production was female dress goods.

The printing of fashion fabrics for women's wear was significantly expanded when William Whiston of Langley Prints Works purchased 90,000 blocks in 1895, with the closure of Baker, Tucker & Co, London, who had been the pre-eminent firm in the trade. Thus, according to Harold Whiston, the print works at Langley went from having only a very secondary place in the home trade to become the first place in the trade dealing with the high class requirements of London, Paris and New York, providing everything in women's dress goods styles that they could long for. This acquisition was followed by others until they were the largest printing works in the world. Not satisfied with the huge range of blocks they now held Harold Whiston, in order to maintain novelty in style and colour, engaged the finest designers in Paris, Lyon, Mulhouse, Zurich and Vienna. The pattern books of the period under Harold Whiston's management reflect this investment in design and demonstrate that Macclesfield was producing highly fashionable dress fabrics in

Exhibition of products for the Duchess of Teck's visit, 1895

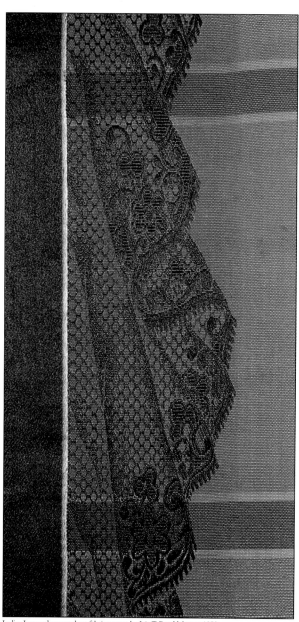

Ladies Jacquard woven dress fabric woven by J & T Brocklehurst c1850

Cut up for a ladies scarf woven by J & T Brocklehurst c1850

Parasol fabric with a velvet border on moire silk woven double width using 2 harnesses c1855

Gum satin Jacquard woven design J & T Brocklehurst c1850

Peter Robinson catalogue 1933

From Silk Journal and Rayon World 1933-34

the early part of the century.

In the second quarter of the 20th century the women's wear fabric for which Macclesfield is perhaps best known is spun silk crepe. This employed a spun silk warp and crepe weft. It was also known as washing or boiling silk, since it was colourfast due to having been boiled in olive oil soap for six hours during the finishing process. Its excellent washing properties, durability and effective marketing established a reputation for the quality of Macclesfield silk which is still remembered today. The most popular designs were colour woven stripes which were of infinite variety in both colour and proportions. In the article titled 'New Styles in Macclesfield Silk' which appeared in the Silk Journal and Rayon World, Doris Hemmings wrote "The Spring collection of Macclesfield Silks has now arrived in the London Offices of Brocklehurst Whiston Amalgamated. Incredible as it sounds this collection of striped silks consists of between 200 and 300 patterns. Their novelty this year is the space-dyed check woven in pure silk; this 'space-dyed' check is more attractive even than the sketch promises it should be, as the colours have been carefully chosen in pastel tints and the space-dying is so accurate that the pattern is kept remarkably regular. In addition to the check, the space-dying is applied to a similar striped design and also to a plain two-colour effect contrasting tone on tone against white or past ground. Marled grounds in 300 different colours and white are shown in "end and end" weave and a similar range of solid colours for trimmings or for the dress itself are also offered. The Brocklehurst Whiston collection thus concentrates on a wide selection of all silk dress materials especially suitable for sports and houseware".

Writing three years later, again in the Silk Journal and Rayon World in an article entitled 'Silks of the Moment' she goes on "All the signs of the times point to a vogue for yarn dyed fabrics in silk during the next couple of seasons and it is not surprising to find as a preliminary that Brocklehurst Whiston Amalgamated have done exceptionally well so far on their Summer trade. Out of their large collection of spun silks they single out 3 numbers on which the colours have concentrated - one of these is a multi-coloured striped material in very gay hues, including a good deal of yellow in the complicated clusters. Another successful design is the very reverse being extremely simple consisting of a wide band, a thin line of white with a ground of colour".

In the archive of Brocklehurst Whiston pattern books and designs that have survived, approximately 1000 paper designs for stripes remain. These are not dated but it could be they were the designs referred to by Doris Hemmings in her articles of the early 1930s. Among the paper designs are some with new strips of braid applied implying that a woven design is introduced into the stripes and indeed in the sample books of Cartwright & Sheldon woven samples of this type survive. The striped designs were produced from the 1920s to the late 1940s and the washing properties of the fast dyed, colour woven, spun crepe led to the reputation for quality and practicality for every day wear. Many of the companies produced stripes and plain fabrics in spun crepe and a number marketed under a particular trade name - the trademark for David Whitfield (which later became part of Brocklehurst Whiston) was Maccleboil, Harry Turner's was Duboil and Cartwright and Sheldon's was Seri Fleur, Hambleton's was Ucanboil.

Dresses and other garments could be purchased either off the peg or made to measure by a local dressmaker. From directory entries and oral history evidence we know that making up firms in Macclesfield were producing dresses and blouses in Macclesfield Stripe, both for private and commercial customers. Madge Dunkerley managed the making up department of Joseph Dunkerley & Son Ltd who employed between 50 and 60 women of which 40 were machinists. They made up garments for private customers and retailers like John Lewis and Harrods. Madge Dunkerley would visit Paris to get ideas for new designs and would buy models each spring and autumn. Cartwright & Sheldon, like many of the other manufacturers, also had a making up department where they fringed and finished neckwear for men as well as women. Macclesfield silk could also be purchased mail order from a catalogue of designs. Leodian of Leodian House, Cockridge Street, Leeds, offered a range of 30 designs of dress with intricate cuts which exploited the qualities of the fabric. The introduction to the catalogue states "All Leodian models are made to measure at prices shown in the catalogue. The workmanship and finish of every garment is subjected to keen scrutiny and is therefore of the highest possible standard. Macclesfield Silk is well known as the most reliable of all silks and we guarantee the silk we sell to wash and wear perfectly".

In addition to its fashion uses spun crepe was also used for blouses, pyjamas, bias scarves and handkerchiefs. Its highly practical washing properties made it particularly suited to the latter and handkerchiefs in a wide variety of colour woven checks and stripes were produced for both men and women. Pattern books of handkerchief designers have survived in the Brocklehurst Whiston books and the Museum collection, established since 1982, contains many examples, some with their trade mark still in place.

In addition to the spun crepe Macclesfield produced a wide variety of printed rayon crepe designs which were marketed alongside the spun silk

With a Satin Stripe.
A new washing silk shirting is used for this neat short-sleeved style with pointed yoke at back and short revers. In ivory/red, ivory/blue and ivory/navy. Sizes 13—14½ .. **39/6**

Sent on Approval

Advertisement c1930

From Silk Journal and Rayon World 1933–34

61

crepes. These were produced by a number of companies including Brocklehurst Whiston and Barracks Printing Works. Both companies printed fashion fabrics on silk and other fabrics for a wide range of clients, including Welch Margetson, Holiday & Brown, Berne Silks, Cresta Silks, Jacqmar and Liberty. In 1954 Barracks Fabrics even printed a small number of designs for Bianchini Ferrier of Lyon. In addition to their many clients outside Macclesfield both Brocklehurst Whiston and Barracks Fabrics also printed for local firms including Edward Lomas, Hambleton and Cartwright & Sheldon.

In the 1980s and 1990s Barracks continue to print for customers like Laura Ashley, Liberty, Betty Jackson, Timney Fowler and Collier Campbell. Adamley Textiles have also woven and printed fabrics for customers like Jean Muir and Ralph Lauren.

Spun crepe Duboil handkerchief, 1930s

Macclesfield Stripe was produced from the 1920s to the 1940s and was extremely popular

Page from the Leodian mail order catalogue

Leodian catalogue cover

Silk Pictures and Ephemera

The earliest known Macclesfield silk picture was of Queen Victoria and Prince Albert woven for The Great Exhibition of 1851 and it is thought that it was produced on a drawloom. It is exceptionally large and intricate, and it is possible that only a small number were manufactured, one of which is in the Museum's collection. The name of J Wilde & Sons, Macclesfield is woven into the picture, but there does not appear to be an entry for the firm in the catalogue of the 1851 Exhibition. However, there is an entry under the firm of Charles Cross, 19 Gutter Lane, Cheapside, which appears to be a description of the same picture. Whether these are one and the same is difficult to establish and as yet there is no known evidence of a link between the two firms.

John Godwin, the Macclesfield designer, designed silk pictures for William Grant of Coventry. These included a series of Boer War personalities, similar to those manufactured at a slightly later date by the better known Thomas Stevens. There are other examples of Victorian bookmarks and silk pictures produced by Macclesfield firms. However, the best known series of silk pictures was started in 1946 when Brocklehurst Whiston Amalgamated produced the A.V.R.O. York as a commemorative item to be given to passengers on the first flight. When this deal did not materialise the resulting silk picture was given to the firm's own customers. The idea was repeated in subsequent years as a calendar and eventually a different scene was produced annually as a decorative picture on a commercial basis. Each picture was presented in a folder with the date of production and with information about the subject and name of the designer and weaver. In the early 1950s three hunting scenes and in the 1980s four local scenes were printed rather than woven, but were never as popular. As a series these pictures have now become collectors items. Other firms produced silk ephemera, in particular Cartwright & Sheldon who designed a calendar depicting St Michael's Church in 1948 and subsequently a series of birds and a group of mixed subjects, including handloom weaving at Paradise Mill and the Iron Bridge, as decorative pictures. Spurcroft, which was established in 1981 by John Collins and Eric Ripley, has recently produced silk pictures using both computerised scanning and hand drafted techniques.

Other ephemera printed on silk include playbills provided for Macclesfield Theatre performances of 'Romeo and Juliet' starring Miss Goddard, and "The Bengal Tiger" for the benefit of the engineers and contractors of the North Staffordshire Railway in 1848. Others include playbills for the 'Beggars Opera' and 'Bohemian Girl' at the Theatre Royal in 1850 and 'A Grand Fashionable Night' at the theatre in 1854.

E. WILSON, SILK MANUFACTURER, MACCLESFIELD.

THE NORTH PIER, BLACKPOOL.

108 Steps, Macclesfield produced by Tie Specialities Ltd., in 1973. Designer S A Horsley

Woven by J Wilde & Sons for The Great Exhibition 1851

Non-Fashion Uses

Macclesfield manufacture is mainly associated with fashion and to a lesser extent furnishing fabrics. However, firms have manufactured a variety of items for both industrial and decorative purposes.

Furnishing fabrics do not represent a major part of Macclesfield products but it is clear from exhibition entries that they were produced by a significant number of manufacturers.

Among the products exhibited at the Great Exhibition in 1851 by J & T Brocklehurst was railway carriage furnishings. At the Royal Jubilee Exhibition held in Manchester in 1887 J O Nicholson exhibited work both from the Furniture Silks Manufacturing Company at Hope Mills and the Macclesfield Embroidery School which he had founded in 1882. The manufacturing company exhibited silk damask and brocades, furniture fabrics in spun silk, Tussah silk and cotton. From the School of Embroidery were hand embroidered portieres, curtains, table cloths and borders upon silk satins, plush and Tussah silks, bed covers, tablecloths, chair backs etc. upon cotton linen and woollen cloths.

By 1895, when the Duchess of Teck visited, Macclesfield the firms exhibited furniture damasks of terracotta satin ground with gold thread brocaded figure and another with a delicate salmon ground with design in white and gold and a revival of a Louis XV brocade. Also exhibited was a length of church silk having a gold ground with coloured lilies of subtle shades warp printed by Wardle of Leek. J O Nicholson exhibited brocades in oriental and conventional designs for furniture (some 54 inches wide). Reddish Brothers and Company of Waters Green exhibited printed silk curtains for drawing rooms, and table cloths. Joseph Smith and Sons (Mellor Brothers) of Sutton, who produced church lace and small wares, exhibited 6" lace monogrammed 'IHS' made for a Manchester firm who dealt especially in ecclesiastical trimmings. Joseph Smith supplied a wide range of trimmings and other narrow fabrics suitable for furnishings. On a smaller scale upholstery trimmings were made by smallware manufacturers like Challinor and Holmes, Smith Brothers, and Davenports, although this aspect of the trade has now ceased in the town.

The silk on the walls of the drawing room at Tatton Hall, Knutsford, was said to have been rewoven in Macclesfield in the 1920s to replace an earlier design. Isolated examples of other furnishing textiles can be found in the pattern books of individual manufacturers. The design firm of Godwins were certainly producing damask designs for napiery to be produced by Dunfermline linen weavers.

In the list produced by the Macclesfield Silk Trade Association around 1929

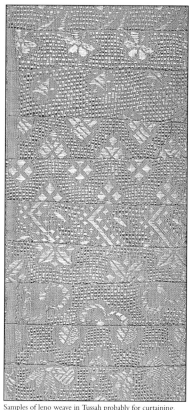

Samples of leno weave in Tussah probably for curtaining.

Jacquard woven altar cloth fabric (church lace) c1940

furnishings are not recorded among the wide range of products produced so it would appear that production was not significant enough to justify an entry.

In the 1940s Barracks were printing upholstery fabrics for Edinburgh Weavers. In recent years Barracks Fabrics have printed and finished a wide range of upholstery fabric in cotton, wool and linen for firms like Liberty, Collier Campbell, Timney Fowler and others.

Mock leno fabrics were manufactured by James Arnold & Co for covering wireless and gramophone speakers and Brocklehurst Whiston Amalgamated manufactured fabric for car upholstery.

In 1895 among the items exhibited by J & T Brocklehurst to celebrate the visit of the Duchess of Teck were "powder bags" in cloth produced in spun silk made for the War Department. During the First World War, the Museum's oral history archive records that "Madge Dunkerley employed 1000 women to make powder bags for munitions". Brocklehurst Whiston Amalgamated are recorded as making balloon cloth and silk was also used for burn dressings amongst other war needs. During the Second World War, the Ministry of Supply: Silk and Rayon Control had its headquarters in Macclesfield. Peter Gaddum of H T Gaddum & Co was responsible for the procurement of raw silk; based in Beirut he travelled widely looking for new sources of supply. Silk was requisitioned for the making of parachutes by selected firms including Cartwright & Sheldon and Brocklehurst Whiston Amalgamated. Later other firms were weaving nylon for the parachutes of bomber crews. Smallware firms manufactured the tapes and cords for the parachutes and military badges. The escape map, printed on silk, was developed and produced in Macclesfield as part of the pilot's emergency kit. A large number of these maps still exist, some having been made into ties, blouses and even dressing gowns.

The early maps were of Western Europe and printed on one side of the cloth, later a technique was developed to print on both sides of the cloth. These double sided maps appear to have predominantly covered the Far East. Intelligence codes were also printed on silk.

In recent years the printing of camouflage fabric for the military has formed a substantial part of Barracks Fabrics' trade and has helped to sustain the firm through difficult times. These fabrics were used in both the Falklands and Gulf Wars.

Other miscellaneous and industrial uses of silk include applications in the flour milling industry for sieves. Silk fishing lines and surgical sutures have now largely been replaced by ones produced with man-made fibres.

Escape Map printed on silk c1944

Propaganda handkerchief

Knitting

Knitting is an industry traditionally associated with the East Midlands in particular the counties of Leicestershire, Nottinghamshire and Derbyshire. However, the production of hosiery, ties, scarves and other knitted fabrics in both silk and man-made fibres was undertaken in Macclesfield. The Universal Directory of 1790 lists a stocking manufacturer in the town at that date. A further reference to a hosiery manufacturer appears in the directories of 1910, but directories for the intervening years do not appear to record this trade.

William Whiston in his somewhat personal account of the history of the Langley Printing Works published privately in the 1940s, records "his pioneering work on the printing of knitted artificial silk fabric". He recalls how in 1914-15 he "established the production of knitted fabrics in Langley using a special type of machinery from Leicester". He even sent Langley girls down to Leicester to learn the craft while the mill was being established. The knitting production at Langley was managed by a Miss Smale to whom Whiston duly gives credit for the success of the enterprise. Artificial silk knitted on both circular and flat bed machines was printed and made up into coats, scarves, jumpers and many other articles of apparel. Despite difficulties in the early months of production Whiston recalls how the success of the enterprise was secured when a Leicester manufacturer bought everything they had for delivery and left a large repeat order. After 3 years of exhausting work he maintained that the capital investment was recovered and they showed a large and satisfactory profit.

In a table drawn up by the Macclesfield Silk Trade Employers Association (circa 1929) eleven manufacturers are listed as engaged in the production of knitted fabrics and garments. These included:- F Bradley & Co., Brough & Co (Macclesfield) Ltd., Cartwright & Sheldon, Challinor & Holmes Ltd., Edward Manufacturing Ltd., John Godwin & Son, T H Hambleton Ltd., A W Hewetson Ltd., A & E Johnson, James Kershaw (Macclesfield) Ltd., Josiah Smale & Son Ltd.

Although the scale of the manufacture of knitted products must have been small in comparison to the production of the East Midlands, yarns for the knitting industry formed a significant part of the Macclesfield silk throwsters' business. It is clear from an article entitled 'Macclesfield Silk Notes' in the Silk and Rayon Journal of August 1930 that knitting yarns helped to sustain the industry when demand for woven yarns were poor. The article states "There is still a great deal of uncertainty as to the future, and although there is slightly improved demand in the knitting section for hosiery yarns there is no improvement in organzine and tram for the weaving trade". Conversely the

18th century hand frame knitter *from Diderot*

Charles Mason c1950 – hand frame knitter at Cartwright & Sheldon

same article in the Silk and Rayon Journal goes on "although in the neckwear trade there is demand for manufactured goods knitting remains dull and the orders are only small". Advertisements for the knitting and hosiery yarns produced by the Macclesfield throwsters appear regularly in the Silk and Rayon Journals of the 1920s and 1930s).

Cartwright & Sheldon made a wide range of knitted products and fabrics in both silk and rayon in the 1920s and 1930s. They employed both hand frame machines for scarves and ties and powered machines for knitted fabric. Knitters were recruited from the Nottingham area. Production ceased when Charles Mason, the last of the handframe knitters employed by them died in the 1950s.

Knitted fabrics continue to be made in the area, on computerised circular machines, by W K Lowe but their production is mainly in cotton man-made fibres and synthetic fibres. Mowbrays process and texturise a wide variety of man-made fibre yarns for use in the knitting and hosiery industry both in this country and abroad.

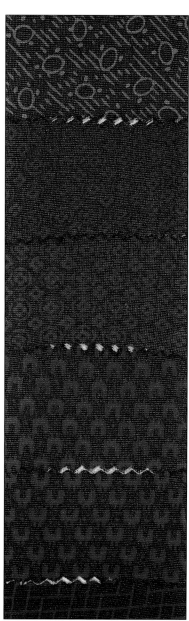

"Sudbury Special" knitted fabric printed at Langley

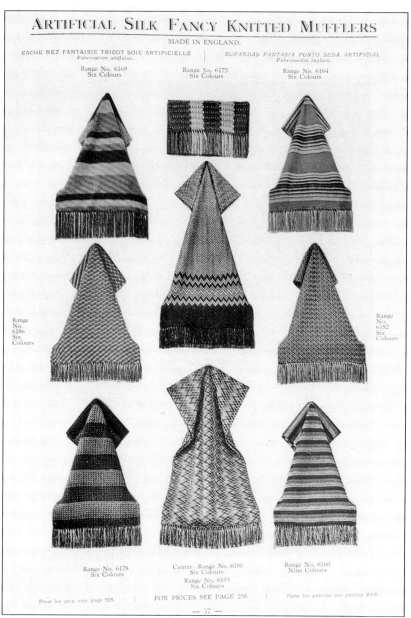

Welch Margetson catalogue c1930

70

Black satin embroidered apron

An embroidered badge

Trimmings

In the 18th century button manufacturers frequently also made smallwares such as galloons, doubles and ferrets. However, there was very little manufacture of ribbons at that time. The Ribbon Weavers Committee Report of 1818 stated in evidence from Peter Keefe, a Macclesfield silk mill manager, that "ribbon weaving was not a significant trade, with less than 20 ribbon looms in the town".

Although Macclesfield is not associated with the production of ribbons in the same way that Coventry, and to a lesser extent Congleton are, several Macclesfield firms did weave ribbons and sashes for dress trimmings in the 19th century and also had substantial trade in braids and other smallwares. In the 20th century embroidery and badge making have been significant industries.

From the pattern books there is evidence that firms like J & T Brocklehurst, J O Nicholson, J & F Jackson and T H Hambleton wove narrow ribbons and wide sashes sometimes with points, fringes and tassels. An interesting combination of techniques was employed including Jacquard weave, ikat, moire and velvet, often more than one technique to a ribbon.

Mellor Brothers, listed in directories as smallware manufacturers was established in 1830. The firm had a reputation for the high quality of its ribbon weaving. It specialised in gold braid weaving for the Admiralty and was one of only two firms in the country which undertook this work. In 1896 this firm produced a bookmark to mark the centenary of the founding of the Macclesfield Sunday School. Mellors was taken over by Peter Davenport, which was established in 1848, and specialised in tassels for umbrellas and other uses, pom-poms, fringes, gimp, wire, clerical and uniform braid and trimmings. Both firms became part of the Berisford Group in 1983.

A W Hewetson, listed as silk embroidery manufacturers and the kindred trades, was founded in 1898 and began with four hand pantograph embroidery machines, adding Schiffli machines in 1905. The type of work undertaken included embroidery on black satin ladies' aprons, winceyette nightdresses, jap silk embroidered underskirts, and from 1925 decorated the neck wear made in its own making-up department. During the two Wars the majority of production was turned over to badges, and in the Second World War 50 million badges were produced. In 1927 automatic machines were installed and the firm claimed to be "the largest manufacturer of all types of embroidery in the world", including badges from football clubs to Masonic lodges, guipure lace, broderie anglaise, fusible motifs and cornelly embroidery. The firm joined the Berisford group in 1982.

Silk Trimming Manufacturers.
Gimps, Fringes, &c.

Bayley Ann, Duke st
Beech Joseph, Sandbrow mill
Bell Nathaniel, Chester st
Boulton Thomas, Mill st
Clark James, Park lane
Clark Ralph, Park lane
Davenport Wm. Chestergt
Fairfax Francis, Bank top
Joul Jph & John, Commongt
Kirkham Rd. King Edward st
Machall Hy. Chestergt
Martin Joseph, Newgate
Moss Brothers, Pickford st
Orme Hy. Fountain st East
Orme Jph. Water cotes
Plant & Slack, King Edwd st
Sharpley & Smith, Royal Depot mills
Sherratt Jph. Ryl Depot mills
Smith James & Son (upholsterer's trimmings) Pitt st
Taylor Matthew, Jordangt
Wadsworth Jph (& silk lace) Sunderland st
Wardle Saml. King Edwd st
Warren Peter, Water cotes
Water Geo. Commongt
Walton & Son, Market pl

Macclesfield Directory 1850

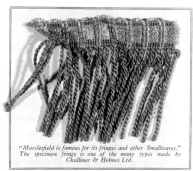

"Macclesfield is famous for its fringes and other Smallwares." The specimen fringe is one of the many types made by Challinor & Holmes Ltd.

Challinor & Holmes Ltd

J O Nicholson, also known as a broad cloth weaver, founded the Macclesfield School of Embroidery to teach embroidery for commercial manufacture; church embroidery for use in local churches was a speciality.

Other firms included Attwell and Jenner, in business from the 1880s to 1980s who used Swiss hand embroidery pantographs and then German Jacquard automatic machines. Smith Brothers was established in 1819, manufacturing upholstery gimps, cords, fancy galloons, fringes and trimmings for canopies, lacing and fancy cords and Challinor and Holmes, established in 1920, produced embroidery threads, braids, fringes, tassels and had extensive trade in silk and rayon hosiery and smallware yarns, flosses and other embroidery twists.

Berisfords, ribbon weavers of Congleton, had premises in Macclesfield for many years and absorbed all the major smallware manufacturers of Macclesfield.

Some embroidery and badgemaking is still carried on in the town, by firms such as Embro, Jem Embroidery and Hewetson Leveaux.

Collections

The patterns of the Macclesfield textile industry have survived in both public and private collections. There are two major public sources and three major private collections held by manufacturers and not accessible for study purposes. The two public collections are held by Macclesfield Museums Trust and Cheshire County Record Office.

The Macclesfield Museums Trust Silk Museum collection comprises the pattern books of the following manufacturers and designers:

Barracks Fabric Printing Company
Incomplete series 1926 – 1966

Brocklehurst Fabrics
Incomplete series 1850 – 1980s

Cartwright and Sheldon
Business records – incomplete 1912 – 1981
Textile sample blankets 1912 – 1981

John Godwin Designers
Mainly scrap books of designs 1840 – 1910

Macclesfield Silk Manufacturing Society
Pattern books series 1890 – 1970
Minute books 1888 – 1920
[Most recent minute books held at Modern Record Centre, University of Warwick]

Collections held by Cheshire County Record Office:

Brocklehurst Whiston Amalgamated
Incomplete series 1840s–1960s

Langley Printing Company
Incomplete series 1840s–1960s

Access by appointment only to both collections

Macclesfield Museums	Cheshire County Record Office
The Heritage Centre	Duke Street
Roe Street	Chester
Macclesfield	CH1 2QP
SK11 6UT	
Tel: 01625 613210	Tel: 01244 602574
Fax: 01625 617880	Fax: 01244 603812

Macclesfield Manufacturers Trademark

Directory of Companies

ADAMLEY TEXTILES LIMITED

1965 –
Sutton Mills and Langley Print Works
also Waller Street Mill

Adamley Textiles was formed in 1965 as a hand block printing business. In order to dye and finish their own cloth the firm moved to Langley about 1970. Handblock printing was gradually superseded by screen printing. In the mid 1970s the Oberland Silk Manufacturing Co was purchased in order that weaving could be incorporated into the business. Facings for men's evening jackets, a speciality of Oberlands, was continued for some time. Some ecclesiastical work was undertaken for a time using the expertise and designs of the East Anglian Weaving Co.

The main products today are both men and ladies fashions using silk which has been woven, dyed and printed in Macclesfield. 60% of the silk produced is exported to America.

Block printer from Book of Trades c1820

BARRACKS FABRIC PRINTING CO

1924 –
Lower Heyes Mill, Black Lane
also Crompton Road

The Company was founded in 1924 by H G Herman as commission silk dyers. In the early years stencil printing was introduced and then handblock printing. The Barracks Co and Langley Printworks were early pioneers in screen printing and Barracks was the first firm to undertake hand screen printing using the photographic process for engraving screens. It became the largest hand screen printers in England.

In 1931 the firm moved from the old military barracks on Crompton Road to larger premises in Lower Heyes Mill.

Block printing was gradually superseded by screen printing and the advent of automatic printing in the 1950s meant that hand screen printing has almost disappeared. Barracks purchased Bauser flat bed screen printing machines and were thus able to apply hand techniques by mechanical means. Hand printing is now only used for sampling, small quantity or specialist work.

The firm has always been innovative and has printed using discharge and resist processes, the cloque process, metallic prints and on flock.

The main areas of production are up market fashion fabrics in synthetics, wools, fine cottons, crepes and some silk; furnishings including chintz cottons, polyester and silk and government contract work for camouflage material. Other products include headscarves, shawls and children's bedding. Silk dyeing has been re-introduced.

In 1964 Barracks became a member of the Courtaulds Group, opening the firm to wider markets and has recently formed even closer links with a sister company, Standfast, who specialise in rotary printing.

BROCKLEHURST FABRICS
1745 – 1991
Hurdsfield Road Mills
also Arbourhay St., Exchange St., Henderson St.

The firm dates from 1745 and has the longest life span of any Macclesfield firm. Acton & Street, button manufacturers, were joined in 1748 by John Brocklehurst, a chapman; Brocklehursts remained connected with the firm until 1911. By the early 19th century the firm was throwing silk and manufacturing silk handkerchiefs, ribbons and broad silk and also specialised in broad silk spinning.

In 1929 J & T Brocklehurst amalgamated with William Whiston & Son and added printing to its range of activities; block printing continued at Langley until 1964 when the Langley Print Works were closed. Screen printing was continued at Hurdsfield Mills.

In the early 1970s Brocklehurst Whiston Amalgamated became part of the Slater Walker Group and was quickly sold on to Bodycote International. The name was changed to Brocklehurst Fabrics and continued until 1991 when the firm closed and the assets were sold. Weisters bought the order books for the corporate tie trade while Adamley Textiles and David Evans took up the print runs.

Pattern cards for Macclesfield silk buttons and some pattern books and other material are in the Museum, other pattern books and archive material are in the Cheshire Record Office.
Firms amalgamated during Brocklehurst's history are:-
c1929 Adam Hind & Son (Bradford and London)
Central Silk Goods Co Ltd, Davis & Andrews (London), William Whiston & Son (Langley), David Whitfield & Co.
1960s Ormerod Bros (Llanishen, Cardiff, Brighouse Yorks).
c1970 Winterthur (Dunfermline), Horrocks.

WILLIAM WHISTON & SON
1826–1929
Langley Print Works
(amalgamated with J & T Brocklehurst and Sons Ltd to form Brocklehurst Whiston Amalgamated 1929)

William Smith commenced hand tie and dye, wax resist and indigo printing on a commercial basis in 1826. The business expanded and diversified and in 1870 passed to William Whiston (a relative) and became known as William Whiston & Son.

Up to 1875 hand tie, wax printing, resist and pad, and plate printing were the four main processes. Silks from abroad were used, for example Indian corahs from Calcutta. Between 1875 and 1895 the main trade was with the Rangoon market, printed on fabrics supplied by Brocklehursts.

In 1895 William Whiston acquired a substantial part of the business of Baker, Tucker and Company and shortly afterwards the Persian and Kashmir patterns from the Swaisland Silk Printing Co., this resulted in the largest collection of blocks in Europe.

William Whiston was one of the first to introduce screen printing in an attempt to print longer runs more economically and was in the forefront of developing artificial silks.

Another innovation was the technique of printing on fabric knitted on either circular looms or flat bed machines.

The firm continued printing as part of Brocklehurst Whiston Amalgamated until 1964 when the hand blocks were disposed of, many were destroyed although some sets were sold intact and the majority are now in the Zucchi collection in Italy.

The pattern books were donated to the Cheshire Record Office. Some archives remain within the Whiston family.

CARTWRIGHT & SHELDON LIMITED
1912 – 1981
Paradise Mills
also Vincent Street Mill and Booths Mill, Poynton

The firm was founded by Arthur Cartwright and Percy Sheldon and always remained a family-run firm. The main product was 28" squares woven on handlooms which remained in limited operation until the firm's closure.

Other fabrics included:- figured cut ups, vestings, gum twills, dressing gown cloth, shirting, Jacquard mufflers, long scarves, washing silk (known as Macclesfield Stripe) and knitted ties and scarves.

There was a large making up department making collars and bows and bias scarves and handkerchiefs printed on a mixture of silk and rayon.

During the Second World War the firm was chosen to weave parachute silk. The early 1950s saw the firm flourishing and still producing silk for the top end of the market, although increasingly turning to synthetic fibres. By the mid 1960s however, business declined and never recovered. In 1984 the top floor of the Lower Mill which housed the handlooms, was opened to the public as a Working Museum by the Macclesfield Sunday School Heritage Centre Trust and is now owned and managed by Macclesfield Museums Trust.

The pattern books were bought by a local firm but the Museum holds a substantial range of fabric samples and some of the business archives. In addition the public is able to see the Jacquard handlooms and other associated machinery and ephemera associated with the firm.

JOHN GODWIN & SON
1820 – c1950
Athey Street Mill
also Ardwick

The firm was founded in 1820 in Ardwick, Manchester and moved to Macclesfield in 1873, becoming one of the largest design firms in the country. The firm designed mainly for the damask trade in Dunfermline and Belfast, with some silk for Macclesfield and towelling and cotton for Lancashire.

About 1908 the fashion for damask table linen declined and was replaced by printed table cloths and napkins.

The firm continued in a much smaller way, designing for the ribbon industry and cotton trade. After the Second World War the firm supplied ties to South America but when the last surviving designer died the design business was transferred to Como.

Other businesses were started; a small firm Fancy Trimmings manufactured tassels, cards and other small wares and became part of Peter Davenports in 1952. Gilton and Godwin manufactured women's nightwear and underwear until 1961 when the business was sold to Cooks of Middlewich who continued trading until 1968.

CARTWRIGHT & SHELDON LTD.

Weavers of:
FINE QUALITY TIE MATERIALS

Manufacturers of:
HANDKERCHIEFS, SQUARES AND SCARVES FOR WOMEN'S WEAR

PARADISE MILLS : MACCLESFIELD
CABLES: SEANDESS, MACCLESFIELD

JAMES ARNOLD & CO

1893 - 1993
Wood Street Mill
also Park Green Mill, Brunswick Mill,
Sunderland Street Mill,
Chapel Street garret houses, London Road Dyeworks

James Arnold founded the firm in 1893, occupying rooms first at Park Green Mill then in more extensive premises at Brunswick Mill, Lowe Street, where there was both hand and powerloom weaving as well as knitting and a making up department. Initially the firm concentrated on weaving and expanded by buying premises and business from John Barlow of Wood Street Mill, trading under the name of Wood Street Silk Manufacturing Co. In 1920 Arnolds took over the London Road Dyeworks where dyeing and hand block printing were carried out until 1972. The firm undertook specialist work in the Chapel Street garrets until about 1950, weaving silk for altar cloths and small orders of reppe weave tie cloth. The firm also had a knitting department and wove Macclesfield Stripe.

In the 1930s Brunswick Mill wove motif ties for universities and the firm was one of the first to build up a business in club ties. After the Second World War Arnold's concentrated in producing ties in man-made fibres for this market.

Arnolds acquired the pattern books from a number of firms, including:- T H Hambleton, J & F Jackson, J Staniforth, J O Nicholson and Tie Silks, originally from Krefeld.

When the firm closed the majority of the pattern books were sold out of the area. The Museum has a large quantity of design drafts.

JOHN BARLOW

1890 - 1913
Wood Street
also Copper Street

John Barlow specialised in mufflers and cut-ups and although operating for only 20 years appears to have had a substantial business. In 1908 plans for an extension to the mill reveal 96 employees. The business and premises were acquired by James Arnold in 1913.

T H HAMBLETON LIMITED

1886 - 1939
Elizabeth Street Mill
also Park Lane, Paradise Mill

The firm of Hambleton & Brown was established in 1886. In 1891 the partners acquired Paradise Mill, letting out part of the mill to James Kershaw and others. T H Hambleton bought out his partner William Brown in 1903. When Joshua Nicholson retired in 1910 he transferred his business to Hambleton who subsequently moved to Elizabeth Street where where the firm continued until 1939. The firm manufactured tie silks, mufflers, cut-ups, scarves and knitted ties.

J & F JACKSON

c1830 – 1924
Sutton Mills
also King Edward Street, Pickford Street, Cross Street

James and Ferdinando Jackson, occupied premises on King Edward Street and Pickford Street before moving to Sutton Mills about 1870. Ferdinando Jackson was instrumental in building the town's waterworks and featured prominently in municipal affairs.

JOHN STANIFORTH

c1870 – c1910
Pool Street (Waller Street)
also Park Lane, Mill Lane

Little is known about this business although the surviving pattern books show many topical patterns, including one of Disraeli. Weaving details include "Plush Swivel". Examples of plain corded handkerchiefs also exist.

J O NICHOLSON

1865 – 1910
Elizabeth Street Mill
also Prestbury Road Mill, Hope Mill

J O Nicholson was a member of a leading silk family of Leek. His father owned Brough, Nicholson & Co of Leek and donated the Nicholson Institute to the town.

Joshua Nicholson started his own business in 1865 and produced silks for a variety of uses including dress, furniture and embroidery. He collaborated with William Morris and promoted artistic excellence in English design, exhibiting at most of the international exhibitions. In 1882 he founded the Macclesfield School of Embroidery to train women for industry and worked closely with the School of Art. He retired in 1910.

Pirn winder etching by R A Riseley

Handloom weaver etching by R A Riseley

JOSIAH SMALE & SON LIMITED

c 1830 - 1989

George Street Mill

also Bollin Mills, Brook Street Mill, Park Lane Mill,
Alma Mill

The firm was founded between 1830 and 1840 by
Josiah Smale. In the 19th century products included:-
figured dress silks, printed foulards, mufflers,
handkerchiefs, tie silks, Madras check surahs, large squares
for ladies headwear and gents tie silks. In 1911 the
grandsons of the founder split the firm into Josiah Smale
& Sons and Jonathan Smale & Bros. The firm of John
Birchenough was incorporated in 1912 and Bradley
Smale who became Managing Director introduced a
large business in knitted neckwear fabrics. The Smale
family connection ceased in 1913. In the 1970s the firm
became part of the Tootals Group specialising in club ties
in man-made fabrics. There are very limited business
archives in the Museum and no known surviving pattern
books.

Macclesfield Silk Manufacturing Society early 20th century

MACCLESFIELD SILK MANUFACTURING SOCIETY

1888 - 1976

London Road Mill

also Pioneer Mill, Henderson Street Mill,
Bond Street Mill

The Macclesfield Silk Manufacturing Society was
registered as a co-operative venture by local handloom
weavers. It specialised in scarfs, cut ups, 28" squares and
mufflers, originally for the high quality end of the
market. Power looms were installed in 1902 and shortly
after, a knitting department. The firm was one of the
leading suppliers of the Macclesfield long scarf. The
Macclesfield Silk Manufacturing Society supplied the
Co-operative Wholesale Society but also dealt directly
with retailers.

In 1956 a making up department and a separate
underwear department were established both of which
proved successful. In 1960 the name of the Society was
changed to Macclesfield Silk and Textiles Limited and in
1967 the weaving department which had been losing
money, closed down. The pattern books are housed in
the Silk Museum with the minute books up to 1926.
The later minutes are deposited in the Modern Record
Centre, University of Warwick.

Glossary of Terms

Armozine heavy plain silk, usually black, used especially for clerical gowns and mourning.

Bandanna a coloured silk or cotton handkerchief or headscarf - originally with white spots

Barathea a fine textured twill cloth

Barcelona (handkerchief) a handkerchief or neckerchief of soft twilled silk

China silk a light plain woven silk fabric

Chine a fabric given a mottled pattern by colouring the warp or weft

Cloque a fabric with an irregularly raised or embossed surface

Corah an Indian pattern silk handkerchief; undyed silk

Crepe a fabric with a crinkled surface

Crepe de chine a fine crepe of silk

Cut up divide by cutting

Damask richly figured woven material (originally silk) with a pattern visible on either side - twilled table linen with woven designs shown by the reflection of the light

Ducape a heavy silk dress fabric

Ferret narrow ribbon, a kind of tape

Figured silk designs in coloured threads woven on the material

Foulard soft light twilled washing silk, for ties and scarfs

Fustian a napped fabric; a mixture of linen and cotton and wool

Galloon trimming braid for uniform, upholstery - made of silk, metal or other thread

Gauze very thin silk, almost transparent

Gros de Naples a silk fabric originally associated with Naples

Grosgrain plain ribbed silk

Ground background of the pattern

Gum used to stiffen textiles

Ieno gauze like fabric

Ikat a technique (from Indonesia) of textile decoration in which warp or weft threads or both are tied at intervals and dyed before weaving

Madder dye a reddish-purple colour

Moire a watered fabric (originally mohair now usually silk)

Pekin a silk textile similar to taffeta, having fine stripes running through it

Persian a thin soft silk usually used for linings

Pongee a soft, usually unbleached type of Chinese silk fabric woven from uneven threads of raw silk

Resist-dyeing process in which wax is applied to the cloth to prevent the dye reaching certain areas and so creating a pattern

Sarsenet a fine soft silk fabric

Satin foulard a silk fabric satined either in stripes or spots

Shirting plain weave, with narrow coloured stripes

Steel A Jacquard fabric for ties woven with a very small design in black, white and grey. Worn on formal occasions and for business, from the late 19th century

Surah tie silk - printed surah is known as foulard

Swivel weaving produces small figure motifs which give the fabric an embroidery appearance

Taffeta thin glossy silk with a wavy lustre

Tie and dye the process in which an area of cloth is secured from colouration by firmly wrapping, tying or stitching it before immersion in a dye

Tussah/Tussore silk wild silk, brownish in colour - imported from India (and China). Much used for dress materials end of 19th century

Twill fabric with a surface of parallel diagonal ridges

Warp-faced term for a fabric with many more warp than weft threads, so that the weft are covered by warp

Selected Further Reading

DYEING & PRINTING

Handblock Printing and Resist Dyeing (1985)   *Bosence S*
An Introduction to Textile Printing (3rd Ed.1971)
                                        Clarke W
A Dictionary of Dyes and Dyeing (1981)   *Ponting K G*
The Art of the Textile Block Maker (1984)   *Storey J*
Dyes and Fabrics (1978)   *Storey J*
Textile Printing (London, 1979)   *Storey J*
Langley (n.d.)   *Whiston H*

SILK

The Silken Glow of Macclesfield   *Brown W H*
The Silk Industry - (Shire Album No.194)   *Bush S*
An Old Silk Family (1947)   *Crozier A*
L'Encyclopedie de la Soie (Paris)   *Diderot*
The Story of Silk (1990)   *Feltwell Dr J*
Silk (Rev. 1993)   *Gaddum P*
Silk Designs of the 18th Century (1990)   *Rothstein N*
The Book of Silk (1993)   *Scott P*
The Silk Book (1951)   *Silk & Rayon Users Assoc.*
The Silk Industry (1921)   *Warner F*

SOCIAL AND HISTORICAL

A History of Macclesfield - 1817   *Corry J*
A History of Macclesfield (1981 Rep)   *Davies C S*
Silk Town 1750-1835   *Malmgreen G*
Practical View of The Silk Trade (1829)   *Prout J*

EDUCATIONAL

Cheshire Museums & Archives
Education Project: Source Books on Silk

JOURNALS

Silk Journal & Rayon World - 1924 –
Textile History - 1971 –

Rules, &c.

FOR

SILK WEAVERS.

—◆—

MACCLESFIELD, FEB. 20, 1826.

Brother Tradesmen,

If there were none but honest men in the world;—if men always acted upon principles of justice and truth, and did unto others as they would others should do unto them, there would be no necessity for men to unite for their common protection and support: but since this is not the case, and because there are Manufacturers, who, if it were not for the liberal examples of others, and being in some measure compelled by their servants, would never give what might be termed a fair price for their work.—In this case it becomes neces-sary that we should unite, in order to keep these men up to the legal prices of the town.— But this is not all, we have our Trade to guard in a political point of view, and if we are not unanimous amongst ourselves, we shall be un-prepared for any attainment whatever: more-